LOVINA EICHER'S A[...]

The Essential Amish Cookbook

EVERYDAY RECIPES FROM FARM *&* PANTRY

"Praise for Lovina Eicher's new cookbook! I devoured it, and kept thinking, 'Oh, I really *must* try that recipe!' Lovina's comments on many of her recipes allowed me a glimpse into her family's lives and added to my enjoyment. I highly recommend this wonderful book!"
—**Georgia Varozza**, author of *The Amish Canning Cookbook* and *The Homestyle Amish Kitchen Cookbook*

"I love this cookbook. I'm honored to endorse any work by Lovina Eicher. Like thousands of others, I am a big fan of hers!"
—**Sherry Gore**, bestselling author of *Me, Myself, and Pie*

"You don't have to be Amish to have many reasons to have *The Essential Amish Cookbook* handy in your own kitchen. A wealth of recipes that have been tested many times when sharing meals with friends and family in her home and with her church family."
—**Lovella Schellenberg**, coauthor of *Mennonite Girls Can Cook*

LOVINA EICHER'S AMISH KITCHEN

The Essential
Amish Cookbook

EVERYDAY RECIPES FROM FARM & PANTRY

Lovina Eicher

Herald Press

Harrisonburg, Virginia

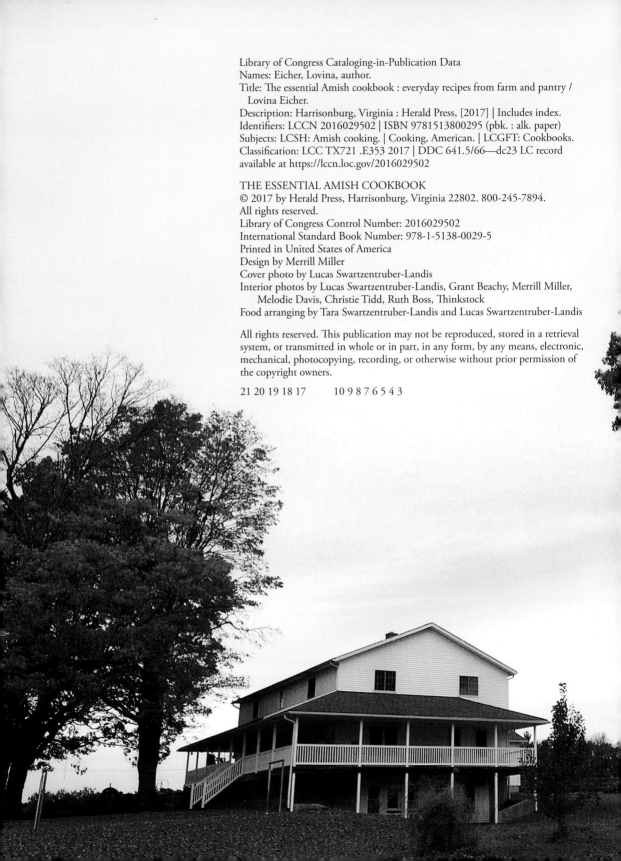

Library of Congress Cataloging-in-Publication Data
Names: Eicher, Lovina, author.
Title: The essential Amish cookbook : everyday recipes from farm and pantry /
   Lovina Eicher.
Description: Harrisonburg, Virginia : Herald Press, [2017] | Includes index.
Identifiers: LCCN 2016029502 | ISBN 9781513800295 (pbk. : alk. paper)
Subjects: LCSH: Amish cooking. | Cooking, American. | LCGFT: Cookbooks.
Classification: LCC TX721 .E353 2017 | DDC 641.5/66—dc23 LC record
available at https://lccn.loc.gov/2016029502

THE ESSENTIAL AMISH COOKBOOK
© 2017 by Herald Press, Harrisonburg, Virginia 22802. 800-245-7894.
All rights reserved.
Library of Congress Control Number: 2016029502
International Standard Book Number: 978-1-5138-0029-5
Printed in United States of America
Design by Merrill Miller
Cover photo by Lucas Swartzentruber-Landis
Interior photos by Lucas Swartzentruber-Landis, Grant Beachy, Merrill Miller,
   Melodie Davis, Christie Tidd, Ruth Boss, Thinkstock
Food arranging by Tara Swartzentruber-Landis and Lucas Swartzentruber-Landis

21 20 19 18 17   10 9 8 7 6 5 4 3

To my husband Joe and my eight children:
Elizabeth, Susan, Verena, Benjamin, Loretta,
Joseph, Lovina and Kevin.

CONTENTS

FOREWORD

*H*ere's something you might not know about the covers of novels written about the Old Order Amish: they're designed to carry a reader into another world. A gentler world, set on a peaceful and pastoral stage, with characters surrounded by a caring community.

As you turn the pages of *The Essential Amish Cookbook* by Lovina Eicher, you'll experience the same reaction. Gorgeous photography—peaceful farm scenery and close-ups of mouthwatering recipes—pulls you in. Read a note or two that Lovina has tucked under the recipes: "Some of our children like to eat peas right from the pod but won't touch them after they're cooked" (Pea and Cheese Salad, page 81). Or "Hobo Suppers make a great dinner when it's hot outside and I don't want to heat up the kitchen. I gather the onions and green bell peppers right out of my garden and we head to the grill. The children help assemble these suppers wrapped in foil" (Hobo Suppers, page 112).

The stressful day you've had starts to recede, you slow down, your imagination soars, your tummy growls. Don't be surprised if you find yourself longing to be a part of this warm and generous family.

And in a way, you can. This cookbook is Lovina Eicher's first solo project (her other Amish Cook cookbooks were coauthored). Through these pages, she's inviting you into her kitchen, garden, family, church, and, well, the essentials of her Amish life. The recipes are filled with her tips, memories, and recommendations, collected from day-to-day experiences.

So dip into this book and begin. Try, enjoy, experiment, learn. And as you cook, don't forget to bring some of those Amish essentials into your own home.

—*Suzanne Woods Fisher*
   Author of Amish Peace: Simple Wisdom for a Complicated World

ACKNOWLEDGMENTS

I would like to thank my husband, Joe, for always encouraging me to keep writing, and for his help with this cookbook. He was willing to help with the outdoor cooking so the photographer could get pictures of food being cooked in a kettle over an open fire or on the grill. My husband's love for outdoor cooking has often saved me from having to make a lot of meals in the house—especially on those hot summer days when it is too hot to have the stove or oven on.

I also appreciate all he does for our children and me. Joe works in an RV (recreational vehicle) factory and still tries to keep everything here cleaned up outside and with the garden. May God bless him for being the wonderful husband and father he is!

Special thanks also go to my eight loving children. They make me proud to be a parent.

Elizabeth, age twenty-two, is happily married to Timothy. She helps me in many ways, especially with my sewing. She is a good, fast sewer. She was also a big help testing these recipes and helping on some days when the photographer was here.

Susan, age twenty, was married in August 2016 to Mose. We are happy to have Mose join the family. Susan has also been a great help with this cookbook by doing other work for me so I could do the book work part of it. Susan loves the outdoors and enjoys training ponies. She also helped cook and bake after she came home from work on days the photographer was here.

Verena, age eighteen, helped all four days with the cooking and baking with the photographer. These were long, hard days of testing lots of recipes, and setting the food up for the photographer. She was a great help.

Benjamin, age seventeen, helped with doing other chores so we could have more time for preparing for the cooking/baking days. He also enjoyed helping to test the food. The boys didn't complain about having extra goodies on hand!

Loretta, age sixteen, was also much appreciated the days the photographer was here. On those days, we baked and cooked all day. She and Verena also washed many dishes and pots and pans.

Joseph, age thirteen, milks our cow, Bessie, every morning and evening, providing milk for the family. Joseph is our "run-errands guy" and does a good job keeping the yard mowed during the summer months. He also enjoyed sampling the food.

Lovina, age twelve, also helped after school with the washing and wiping of many, many dishes on the cooking/baking days. She saves many steps for me and is growing up so fast.

Kevin, age ten, likes to help bake cookies if he isn't busy helping his brothers. He also likes mixing cakes together. And of course he loves trying all the goodies we had on the photographer days.

So I owe each of my children a big thank you for their help and patience through the days of preparing for this cookbook. During all this we also prepared for the weddings of our two oldest daughters, Elizabeth and Susan.

I also owe a big thank you to the editors at MennoMedia. Without their help, this cookbook would not have been possible.

And last but not least, I owe a special thank you to my great friend Ruth Boss. I will be forever grateful for her help and encouragement. Without her help, I probably would have given up on the column a long time ago. She has been with me every step of the way. I will never be able to repay her for all she has done, but that is a good example of what friends are for. Thank you, Ruth. May God bless you for all you do for others!

And not only did Ruth help, she also gathered her church friends and family together to test all the recipes to make sure they would be just right for all of you to enjoy. Some of them I never met, but they include, alphabetically: Jean Abbott, Judy Alderden, Audrey Bendle, Jane Bolkema, Kristin Bolkema, Diane Bonnema, Marcia Bosma, Tricia Boss, Jana Brandenburger, Andrea Brown, Yvette Chicas, Martha De Jong, Esther De Vries, Laura De Young, Kristin Freel, Jessica Jabaay, Jo Janke, Mary Lagerway, Rachel Lagestee, Sue Lagestee, Lyda Meyer, Angela Oldenkamp, Mary Paulton, Jori Pittman, Ponce Rossi, Kathy Sliekers, Christie Tidd, Terita Turner, Joan Van Drunen, Rachel Wooley, Hannah Yates, and Ruth Zandstra. Thank you so much.

May God bless each of you as you prepare food for your family or loved ones.
—*Lovina Eicher*

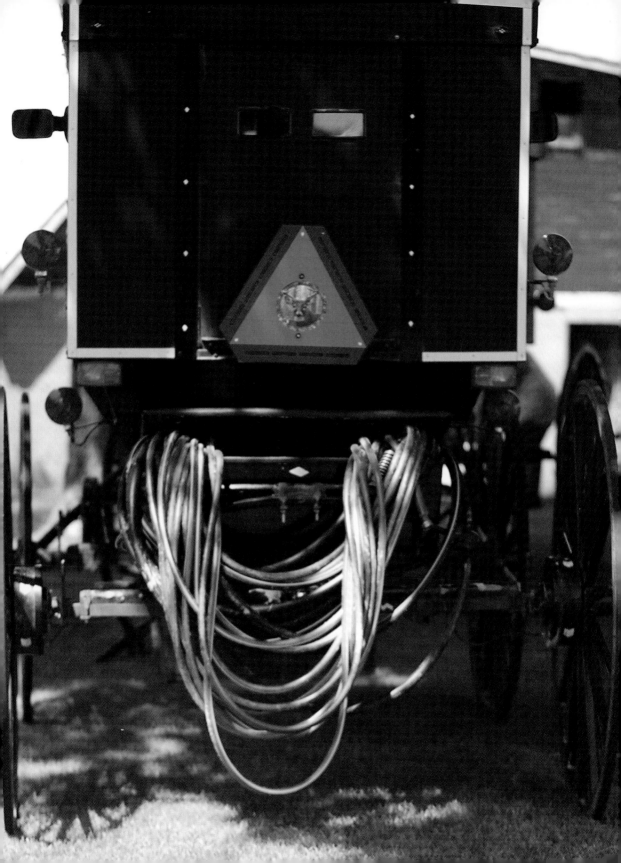

INTRODUCTION

*L*ife has brought lots of changes since I started penning my column in 2002. I started writing under the name The Amish Cook. Then in 2014, due to some unfortunate circumstances, I was blessed to have the editors at MennoMedia help me continue on with this column under the name Lovina's Amish Kitchen, as it remains today. They have been very helpful to me!

We are grateful for all the newspapers who share this column every week with their readers.

The editors at Herald Press wanted me to try my hand at making a cookbook on my own for the first time. I am coauthor of previous cookbooks, such as *The Amish Cook at Home*, *The Amish Cook's Baking Book*, *The Amish Cook's Anniversary Book*, and *Amish Cooks across America*. This project has been an exciting adventure, although I could not have done it without the help of many others.

Let me also mention that my dear mother, Elizabeth Coblentz, started penning The Amish Cook eleven years before I took over. I was a teenager at home when Mom started writing. Quite often one of my sisters or I would rewrite the column into her notebook so she would have a copy of her writings. I imagined Mother still writing years down the road, but God had other plans. My mother passed away suddenly at the age of sixty-six. My father had passed away, also unexpectedly, a few years before that, at age sixty-nine. Life seemed lonely without my parents.

I am the fourth daughter out of the six girls in our family, and I was encouraged to continue writing Mom's column. I was nervous, as I didn't consider myself a writer like my mother. But in honor of her, I wanted to try.

I find peacefulness when I write these columns. Somehow putting on paper the good and bad happenings in life clears my mind. It is hard to explain. I couldn't do this without asking God to guide my thoughts as I continue writing. There are times I do not know when I sit down to write what I will come up with. There are weeks when it seems as though the same things are happening in our lives over and over, and that is what I share. So to all my readers—I hope you can excuse me if you think that happens!

I was born May 22, 1971, to very dear parents, Ben and Elizabeth Coblentz. I couldn't have asked for better parents. They set a good example for my seven siblings and me. When I was twenty-two years old, I married my most kind and thoughtful husband, Joe. Joe and I are blessed with eight children. God has been good to us.

I learned to cook from my mother at a young age. I liked to sit and watch her mix bread dough. She had a hand-cranked bread mixer, and we would turn it for her sometimes. If she made pie dough, she would give us a small piece to roll out. We would have lots of fun trying to roll out a crust. Mom would sprinkle sugar on it and bake it, and then we ate it. That was all good practice.

Since Amish cookbooks are often full of delicious desserts, as I share in these pages, I do want to say that we grew up mostly only having dessert when company came, or for Sunday dinners. I do the same with my family. We only have dessert on special occasions and when we have company. We do keep homemade cookies on hand for snacks or a light dessert most of the time.

This cookbook is called *The Essential Amish Kitchen*, and while no one cook or person can make an official list, I will share the essentials I always like to keep on hand when I cook. These are ingredients such as flour, sugar (powdered, brown, and granulated), salt, vanilla, baking powder, baking soda, spices, butter, yeast, and more.

I also consider eggs and milk to be essential, and we're so happy to have a cow and chickens so that we have our own milk and eggs on hand. We raise butchering chickens every year for meat, as well as our own beef and pork. So we always have meat in the freezer.

Our garden also provides us with all the vegetables, both fresh and preserved, that we need every year. Some of the vegetables are canned and some are frozen. We also freeze and can peaches, pears, and applesauce, and make juices from grapes and rhubarb. We grow spearmint and peppermint to make our own tea with. Tea leaves can be dried or steeped and frozen in concentrate form for winter use.

While there are many additional foods we buy at bulk food stores and groceries, I hope this book will provide recipes that are easy to follow using the basic essentials that most cooks keep on hand every day.

May God bless you as you try your hand at cooking, and may you enjoy using this book!

Quick Breads & Yeast Breads

APPLESAUCE NUT BREAD

1 cup sugar

1 cup applesauce

2 eggs

¼ cup vegetable oil

3 tablespoons milk

2 cups flour

1 teaspoon baking soda

1 teaspoon baking powder

½ teaspoon salt

½ teaspoon ground cinnamon

½ cup nuts, chopped

In a bowl, mix the sugar, applesauce, eggs, oil, and milk until well blended. In a medium bowl, stir together the flour, baking soda, baking powder, salt, and cinnamon. Add flour mixture to applesauce-egg mixture and mix until well blended. Stir in nuts.

Pour batter into a greased 9 x 5 x 3-inch loaf pan. Bake at 350°F for 60–70 minutes, or until toothpick inserted in center comes out clean.

Cool about 10 minutes in pan, then remove from pan and continue cooling on wire rack.

When I was growing up, we had our own apple trees. The Golden Delicious apples were the ones Mom used to make applesauce.

The apple trees were nice climbing trees, but we weren't allowed to climb them when there were apples on them. Mom didn't like it when we had church services at our house during the time apples were ripe—it was a trial to try to keep the children out of the trees.

Macintosh and Golden Delicious apples made the best applesauce. I usually use 2–3 bushels of apples each fall to make applesauce. The applesauce in this recipe makes the bread more moist.

BANANA ZUCCHINI BREAD

4 eggs, beaten

1 cup vegetable oil

2 cups sugar

2 medium bananas, mashed (1 cup)

3 cups flour

1½ teaspoon baking powder

1½ teaspoon baking soda

1½ teaspoon ground cinnamon

1 teaspoon salt

1½ cup zucchini, unpeeled and shredded

1 cup pecans, chopped

In a large bowl, mix together eggs, oil, and sugar. Add bananas and mix well.

In a separate bowl, stir together flour, baking powder, baking soda, cinnamon, and salt.

Add flour mixture to egg mixture and mix until combined. Stir in zucchini and pecans.

Pour into two greased 9 x 5 x 3-inch loaf pans. Bake at 350°F for 50 minutes, or until toothpick inserted in center comes out clean.

Cool in pan on rack for 10 minutes. Remove bread from pan and cool completely.

Zucchini bread with a taste of banana and pecans makes a good-tasting bread. I like a slice of fresh zucchini bread with coffee.

BLUEBERRY BANANA BREAD

2 cups sugar
½ pound butter or margarine, melted
2 eggs
2 teaspoons vanilla extract
3 cups flour
2 teaspoons baking soda
¼ teaspoon salt
4 mashed bananas, plus milk to measure 3 cups
2 cups blueberries

In a medium bowl, cream together sugar and melted butter or margarine. Add eggs and vanilla and mix well. Add flour, baking soda, salt, and bananas-milk mixture; mix until combined. Fold blueberries into batter.

Spoon batter into two greased and floured 9 x 5 x 3-inch loaf pans. Bake in preheated 350°F oven for 50–55 minutes, or until toothpick inserted in center comes out clean.

Cool in pans for 10 minutes before turning out onto a rack. Makes two loaves.

We have several U-pick blueberry fields that are a few miles from us, so it is easy to get fresh blueberries in our area.

CARAMEL PECAN ROLLS

2¼ teaspoons (1 package) active dry yeast
¼ cup warm water (110°F–115°F)
1¼ cup milk
⅓ cup butter, melted
¼ cup granulated sugar
1 teaspoon salt
2 eggs, beaten
5 cups bread flour, divided

Topping
¾ cup pecans, chopped
1 cup granulated sugar
1 teaspoon ground cinnamon
½ cup butter, melted

Filling
¼ cup butter, softened
½ cup granulated sugar
2 teaspoons ground cinnamon

Caramel sauce
⅔ cup brown sugar, packed
¼ cup butter
¼ cup heavy cream or evaporated milk

In a small bowl, dissolve yeast in warm water. Let stand until creamy, about 10 minutes. Heat milk to lukewarm; pour into a mixing bowl, along with the yeast liquid. Add melted butter, granulated sugar, and salt. Add beaten eggs. Add 3 cups flour and beat on medium speed for 3 minutes. Add remaining 2 cups flour and stir to combine. Remove from mixing bowl and knead until soft and smooth, about 8 minutes. Lightly oil a large bowl, place the dough in the bowl, and turn to coat with oil. Cover with plastic wrap and let rise in a warm place until doubled in size (about 45 minutes).

Prepare filling ingredients: Set out ¼ cup butter to soften. Combine granulated sugar and cinnamon in a small bowl; reserve. Separately, prepare topping: Stir all the topping ingredients together; reserve.

Make caramel sauce: In a small saucepan, bring the brown sugar, butter, and cream to a boil. Cook, stirring, for 3 minutes. Pour into a 9 x 13-inch baking pan. Sprinkle reserved topping on top.

Once dough has doubled in size, cut in half and roll each half into a 12 x 15-inch rectangle. Spread with softened ¼ cup butter. Sprinkle reserved cinnamon sugar over butter. Roll up dough from one long side; pinch seams and turn ends under. Cut each roll into six slices. Place slices in pan, cut side down. Cover and let rise in a warm place until nearly doubled, about 30 minutes. Bake at 350°F for 30–35 minutes, or until golden brown. Let cool 1 minute; invert onto a serving platter.

If you like pecans, you will like these rolls. Some of our children like nuts, and some don't care for them at all.

CINNA-PAN ROLLS

2¼ cups warm water

4½ teaspoons (2 packages) active dry yeast

3 tablespoons granulated sugar

1 tablespoon salt

3 tablespoons shortening

5½–6 cups flour (bread flour recommended)

½ cup butter, melted

1 cup brown sugar, packed

4 teaspoons ground cinnamon

Icing

2 cups powdered sugar

3 tablespoons milk

1 tablespoon butter, melted

1 teaspoon vanilla extract

Pour the warm water into a large bowl and sprinkle the yeast on top. Let stand 1 minute. Add the granulated sugar, salt, shortening, and flour, and stir until well blended. Knead for a few minutes. On a lightly floured surface, roll out dough into a rectangle shape about ½ inch thick.

Spread melted butter over the surface of the dough, then sprinkle on the brown sugar and cinnamon. Slowly roll the dough the long way, being careful not to roll too tight.

Cut the roll into ½-inch slices. Place in two 9 x 13-inch greased pans, with rolls touching. Cover with a damp kitchen towel and place somewhere warm, away from any drafts. Let rise until doubled in size, about 45 minutes.

Bake at 375°F for 20 minutes, or until golden brown.

Make icing: In a bowl, stir together the powdered sugar, milk, melted butter, and vanilla. If too thick, add a few more drops milk. Spread icing over warm rolls.

Makes 30 rolls.

These are similar to cinnamon rolls. They are great with breakfast or for a snack.

HOMEMADE BREADSTICKS

1 cup warm water
1 tablespoon yeast
2 tablespoons sugar
1 teaspoon salt
2 tablespoons vegetable oil
2½ cups bread flour
Butter, melted
Garlic powder
Parmesan cheese
Dried parsley

Mix together warm water, yeast, sugar, salt, and oil. Let stand for a few minutes. Add flour, mix thoroughly, and then let rise for 25 minutes. Roll dough out onto a large baking sheet. Use a pizza cutter to cut into strips. Let rise for a few more minutes. Bake at 350°F for 15–20 minutes, or until lightly browned. Brush with melted butter and sprinkle with garlic powder, Parmesan cheese, and dried parsley. Good when dipped in warm cheese sauce.

Makes 16 regular or 24 smaller breadsticks.

We like breadsticks when we make homemade pizza or pizza casserole. It is an easy recipe to follow.

LIGHT AND TASTY BISCUITS

2 cups flour
2½ teaspoons baking powder
½ teaspoon salt
⅓ cup shortening
¾ cup milk
¼ cup butter, melted

Preheat oven to 475°F. Sift together flour, baking powder, and salt. Cut in shortening with fork until mixture resembles coarse cornmeal. Add the milk and mix lightly with fork only until flour is moistened and dough pulls away from sides of the bowl.

Turn out onto lightly floured board. Knead lightly and roll out ¾ inch thick. Cut out with floured 2½-inch biscuit cutter or juice glass. Re-roll excess dough and cut out remaining biscuits. Place on lightly greased baking sheet, brush tops with melted butter, and bake for 12–15 minutes, or until golden brown.

This is a simple and easy biscuit to make. We like biscuits with homemade sausage gravy.

I've made these biscuits ever since I've been married; another recipe for biscuits I use has mayonnaise in them—we call them "mystery biscuits."

LONG JOHN ROLLS

1 cup lukewarm water

4½ teaspoons (2 packages) active dry yeast

1 cup milk

2 large eggs, beaten

½ cup butter or margarine, softened

⅔ cup sugar

½ teaspoon salt

Pinch ground nutmeg

6–7 cups bread flour

Vegetable oil, for frying

Frosting

⅓ cup shortening or butter

4 cups powdered sugar, divided

1 teaspoon vanilla extract

½ cup milk

In a small bowl, mix the water and yeast. Let stand until creamy, about 10 minutes. Scald the milk and let cool to lukewarm. Add the cooled milk to the dissolved yeast. Stir together eggs, butter or margarine, sugar, salt, and ground nutmeg until well mixed, then add this to the milk-yeast mixture. Gradually add flour until the dough is elastic and easy to handle. Knead until a round ball is formed.

Lightly oil a large bowl, place the dough in the bowl, and turn to coat with oil. Cover with plastic wrap and let rise in a warm place until doubled in size, about 2 hours. Divide the dough in two. Roll out each half to ¾ inch thickness. Cut into 7-inch rectangular pieces. Let rise again, covered with plastic wrap.

Pour vegetable oil into a deep pan to a depth of 2–3 inches. Using a candy thermometer, heat the oil to 400°F. Fry the rolls in batches until golden, 2 minutes on each side.

Make frosting: Cream together shortening, 1 cup powdered sugar, and vanilla. Gradually add the milk and the rest of the powdered sugar, beating constantly. More powdered sugar can be added to give desired thickness. Spread over rolls as desired.

This is a tried-and-true recipe. My mother made Long John Rolls all the time. I also make these often, and they never last long around here. They taste better when eaten within a day or two of making them.

LOVINA'S HOMEMADE BREAD

2¼ teaspoons (1 package) active dry yeast
2½ cups lukewarm water
¼ cup lard or shortening
2 tablespoons sugar
1 tablespoon salt
6 cups bread flour (Lovina uses Robin Hood brand)
Butter, for brushing

In a large bowl, dissolve the yeast in lukewarm water. Stir in lard or shortening, sugar, and salt until well combined. Add the flour, ½ cup at a time, until the dough is elastic and doesn't stick to the sides of the bowl. If it becomes too hard to stir, place on lightly floured surface and knead in the last bit of flour. You may not need to use all 6 cups of flour. Lightly oil a large bowl, place the dough in the bowl, and turn to coat with oil. Cover with plastic wrap and let rise in a warm, draft-free place until doubled in size, about 1 hour. Punch down the dough and let it rise again.

Place the dough on a slightly floured surface and knead for a few minutes. Divide dough into two portions and place in two greased 9 x 5-inch loaf pans. Let rise again.

Bake at 350°F for 30 minutes, or until golden brown around edges. Remove from oven. Brush the tops with butter to keep crusts from getting hard. Let cool, or slice and serve while still warm.

I have made a lot of bread recipes, but this is still my favorite. It was the first bread recipe I made. It was the one my mother always used, and she taught me how to make it. Now, as my oldest daughter is married and cooking without Mom around, she says, "Mom, it doesn't look like yours." But it takes time to get the feel of how the dough should be. Sometimes different flours bake differently; it is also important not to have your flour in a cold room, or to freeze it. If you do keep it somewhere cold, bring it to room temperature before using it to make bread, because that can affect how it rises.

PEACH MUFFINS

1½ cup flour

½ cup granulated sugar

2 teaspoons baking powder

1 teaspoon ground cinnamon

¼ teaspoon salt

1 egg, beaten

½ cup butter, melted

¼ cup milk

2 cups peaches, peeled, pitted, and chopped

Topping

⅓ cup brown sugar, packed

1 teaspoon ground cinnamon

¼ cup flour

2 tablespoons butter, melted

In a large bowl, stir together flour, granulated sugar, baking powder, cinnamon, and salt. Add egg, melted butter, and milk, and beat on medium speed until well blended. Stir in peaches.

Grease and flour a muffin tin, or use paper liners. Fill muffin cups evenly with batter.

In a small bowl, stir together topping ingredients with fork until crumbly. Top muffins with crumb topping.

Bake at 400°F for 20–25 minutes.

We always buy several bushels of peaches each fall. We like to freeze some and also preserve some by canning them.

REFRIGERATOR ROLLS

⅔ cup canola oil

1 tablespoon salt

2 cups warm water

4½ teaspoons (2 packages) active dry yeast, dissolved in ¼ cup warm water

¼ cup sugar

½ cup wheat germ

2 eggs, beaten

6 cups bread flour

Mix oil, salt, water, dissolved yeast, sugar, wheat germ, and eggs in a large bowl. Using a mixer, add flour, 1 cup at a time, and beat on low after each addition until dough gets sticky and too thick for mixer. Stir in the rest of the flour by hand.

Place the dough in a greased large bowl. Cover tightly with plastic wrap. Place in refrigerator for at least 4 hours before forming rolls.

To bake, pinch off dough into 2-inch balls, or scoop out with ice cream scoop. You may need to flour your hands to work with the dough. Place the balls of dough in a greased 9 x 13-inch baking pan about 1 inch apart. Cover with damp cloth and let rise until doubled in size. Don't worry if they don't completely rise; they will pop up when you put them in the oven to bake.

Bake at 375°F for 15–20 minutes, or until golden brown.

Makes two 9 x 13-inch pans, with 12 dinner rolls in each pan.

This is a good recipe to make and store in the refrigerator. If you only want to bake a few rolls at a time, you can leave the rest of the dough refrigerated for up to 5–6 days.

RHUBARB COFFEECAKE

½ cup butter or margarine

1½ cup brown sugar

1 egg

2 cups all-purpose flour

1 teaspoon baking soda

½ teaspoon salt

1 cup sour cream

3 cups rhubarb, washed thoroughly and chopped

Topping

¼ cup granulated sugar

½ cup brown sugar

1 tablespoon butter

½ cup pecans, chopped

In large mixing bowl, cream together butter or margarine, brown sugar, and egg. In another bowl, combine flour, baking soda, and salt. Add to the butter mixture, alternating with the sour cream. Fold rhubarb into batter. Spread into a greased 9 x 13-inch baking pan.

Make topping: In a small bowl, mix granulated sugar and brown sugar. Cut in butter until mixture resembles coarse cornmeal. Stir in pecans. Sprinkle over batter.

Bake at 350°F for 45–50 minutes, or until a toothpick inserted in center of cake comes out clean.

If rhubarb isn't in season, blueberries could be substituted.

Rhubarb is one of the first things that peeps out of the ground in the spring. In the fall, we put manure over the plants and then rake it off before the rhubarb shoots come up in the spring.

SOFT PRETZELS

2 cups warm water

2 tablespoons active dry yeast

¼ cup butter, melted

½ cup brown sugar, packed

2 teaspoons salt

1½ cup whole wheat flour

5 cups all-purpose flour

Butter, for topping, melted

Kosher salt, for topping

In a small bowl, stir together warm water and yeast. Let stand until creamy, about 10 minutes. Add butter, brown sugar, and salt, mixing well. Add whole wheat flour and mix thoroughly. Add enough all-purpose flour to make a soft, elastic dough (you may not need all the flour).

Knead the dough for 10 minutes. Lightly oil a large bowl, place the dough in the bowl, and turn to coat with oil. Cover with plastic wrap and let rise in a warm place until doubled in size, about 1 hour.

When dough has risen, turn out onto a lightly floured surface and divide into 12 to 18 equal-sized pieces. Roll each piece into a rope and twist into a pretzel shape. Place pretzel on a well-greased baking sheet.

Bake immediately at 450°F for 10–15 minutes, or until golden brown. Brush with melted butter and sprinkle with kosher salt.

Good served with cheese sauce.

We like to eat soft pretzels when they are still warm. We dip them in ranch dressing or melted cheddar cheese. We also like to serve them with soups. They make a good snack even if they are cold.

ZUCCHINI CHOCOLATE CHIP BREAD

3 cups all-purpose flour

2 cups sugar

3 teaspoons ground cinnamon

1 teaspoon baking soda

1 teaspoon salt

½ teaspoon baking powder

3 eggs

1 cup canola oil

3 teaspoons vanilla extract

2 cups zucchini, peeled or unpeeled and shredded

1½ cup semisweet chocolate chips

1 (8-ounce) can unsweetened crushed pineapple, drained

In a large bowl, combine the flour, sugar, cinnamon, baking soda, salt, and baking powder. In a small bowl, whisk the eggs, oil, and vanilla. Stir into flour mixture until just moistened. Fold the zucchini, chocolate chips, and pineapple into mixture.

Pour batter into two greased 8 x 4-inch loaf pans. Bake at 350°F for 60–65 minutes, or until a toothpick inserted near the center comes out clean. Cool for 10 minutes before removing from pans to wire racks.

Note: I like to leave the peel on the zucchini when they are fresh from the garden. If the zucchini get too large, sometimes I find the skin is a little bitter. Also, store-bought zucchini sometimes have a wax coating that makes it necessary to peel the skin.

When the zucchini is plentiful in the gardens, it's not unusual to see signs reading "FREE ZUCCHINI" along the roadside in front of Amish homes.

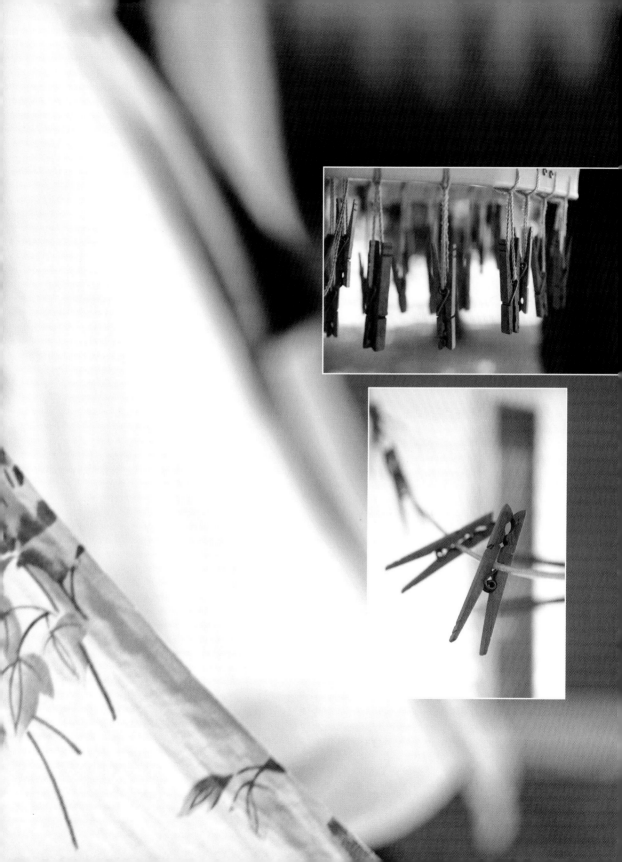

Breakfast Foods

APPLE OVEN PANCAKES

2 tart apples, peeled, cored, and thinly sliced
¼ cup brown sugar, packed
¾ teaspoon ground cinnamon
¾ cup flour
¼ teaspoon salt
3 large eggs
¾ cup milk
1 teaspoon vanilla extract
3 tablespoons butter, melted and divided

Preheat oven to 425°F. Put an oven-safe 9- or 10-inch skillet in the oven.

In a bowl, combine the apple slices, brown sugar, and cinnamon. Toss gently to coat well. In another bowl, mix the flour with the salt. In a small bowl, whisk together the eggs, milk, vanilla, and 1 tablespoon melted butter. Add to flour mixture and stir until combined.

Take the pan from the oven and add the remaining 2 tablespoons butter to it. Swirl to coat the bottom of the pan. Arrange the apple slices in the bottom of the pan. Pour the batter over the apple slices. Bake at 425°F for 25–30 minutes until cooked and lightly browned.

Can be topped with a little powdered sugar or syrup.

The first time I made these pancakes was in home economics in middle school. We had to divide into groups and follow the directions for the recipe. After each group made theirs, we could eat the pancakes. I enjoyed the class; it was at the end of the day when we were always hungry.

The teacher would go through the whole recipe with us, and taught us to never start cooking until you have all your ingredients out.

She had us use china and taught us how to set a proper table. I'm so glad I took that class: when I help with weddings, I know where the fork, knife, and spoon should go. In the Amish lifestyle we don't really learn to do that, but I learned it in home economics in a public school. Nowadays, most of the Amish children go to Amish schools and there are not classes in this kind of thing at the school.

I made this recipe for my family a few times before I was married.

BAKED OATMEAL

½ cup butter, melted; or ¼ cup applesauce

2 eggs, beaten

1 cup milk

3 cups quick-cooking oats

¾ cup brown sugar

2 teaspoons baking powder

1 teaspoon salt

2 teaspoons vanilla extract

2 teaspoons ground cinnamon

Mix all ingredients together in bowl. Pour into greased 2-quart baking dish (or a 9 x 13-inch baking pan). Bake 350°F for 40 minutes.

For added flavor, after the oatmeal is baked, top with any combination of chopped fresh fruit, such as apples, peaches, or strawberries, as well as raisins and chopped pecans or walnuts. We sometimes like to pour cold milk over the top when serving.

Makes 8–12 servings, depending on portion size.

My dad had oatmeal almost every day for breakfast. I do not care for the taste of oatmeal, but a few of our children like it, so we have it once in a while.

BREAKFAST CASSEROLE

6 eggs

2 cups milk

1 teaspoon salt

1 teaspoon ground pepper

1 teaspoon garlic powder

6 slices bread, cubed

1 pound sausage or bacon, cooked, drained, and crumbled

½ cup onions, finely chopped

2 cups cheese, shredded and divided (cheddar or Colby work well)

Beat together eggs, milk, salt, pepper, and garlic powder. Add bread, cooked sausage or bacon, chopped onion, and 1 cup cheese. Pour into a greased 9 x 13-inch pan and bake for 45 minutes at 350°F. When almost done baking, sprinkle remaining 1 cup cheese on top.

This casserole can be made the evening before and refrigerated. I make this a lot the evening before church on Sundays. We like Colby cheese on ours. As soon as I get up on Sunday morning, I'll put the casserole that I prepared the night before in the oven. While everyone is getting dressed for church, our breakfast is getting ready. We have our own milk, eggs, and sausage, so I always have the ingredients on hand. This casserole is also a good way to use up older bread.

BREAKFAST PIZZA

Crust

2 cups flour

½ teaspoon salt

2 teaspoons baking powder

½ teaspoon cream of tartar

½ cup shortening

1 egg

⅔ cup milk

Toppings

10 eggs, scrambled and seasoned to taste

1 pound breakfast sausage, cooked and drained

¼ cup onion, diced

½ cup salsa

2 cups cheddar cheese, shredded (or any favorite cheese)

In a bowl, mix together the flour, salt, baking powder, cream of tartar, and shortening with a fork until crumbly. In a separate bowl, stir the egg and milk together, then add to the flour mixture and stir until a dough is formed. Press into a pizza pan or a 9 x 13-inch baking pan. Bake at 375°F for 10 minutes.

Put toppings on prebaked crust, ending with cheese on top. Bake an additional 20 minutes, or until crust is golden brown.

Additional toppings such as green pepper, olives, and mushrooms, can be added.

Our family likes extra toppings on this pizza. They love when I make a pot of sausage gravy to eat with this pizza.

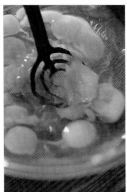

EGG DUTCH

5 eggs
1 teaspoon salt
Ground pepper, as desired
1 heaping tablespoon flour
1 cup milk
1 cup cheese, shredded (any kind works)
Bacon bits, cooked (optional)

In a bowl, beat together eggs, salt, pepper, flour, and milk. Pour into a heated, greased skillet and cover with a tight lid. Place over medium-low heat.

Cut into four pie-shaped pieces and turn each piece over when mixture begins to set and bubble, and finish cooking. Top with shredded cheese when almost cooked through. Add bacon bits, if desired.

This is a breakfast favorite in our family. It's really easy to make. We prefer Colby cheese on top. I double or triple this recipe and divide it into two skillets.

FRENCH TOAST (OVERNIGHT) CASSEROLE

1 loaf white bread

8 eggs

3 cups milk

7 teaspoons sugar, divided

1 teaspoon vanilla extract

¾ teaspoon salt

2 tablespoons butter

2 teaspoons ground cinnamon

Cube bread into 1- to 2-inch pieces and put in buttered 9 x 13-inch baking pan. Beat together eggs, milk, 4 teaspoons sugar, vanilla, and salt, and pour over bread. Cover and let stand in refrigerator overnight, or for 8–12 hours.

When ready to bake, dot butter over top.

Mix together remaining 3 teaspoons sugar and cinnamon and sprinkle over top. Cover and bake at 350°F for 40–45 minutes, removing cover for the last 15 minutes. Serve with maple syrup.

This is an easy way to make French toast when you are limited on time. With our big family, it takes a while to fry enough slices of French toast, so this speeds it up. We love it with our own maple syrup!

FRIED CORNMEAL MUSH

4 cups water, divided
1 cup white cornmeal
1 teaspoon salt
2 tablespoons vegetable oil
Maple syrup (optional)

Bring 3 cups water to a boil in large saucepan. In a bowl, mix together the cornmeal, salt, and remaining 1 cup water. The mixture will be very thick and grainy. Add this mixture to the boiling water and stir until it returns to boiling. The mixture will still be grainy.

Cook for 15–20 minutes, stirring occasionally, until the mush is very thick. Pour the mixture into a 9 x 5-inch loaf pan. Cover and refrigerate overnight, or 8–12 hours.

To fry, heat the oil in a skillet over medium heat. Slice the refrigerated cornmeal into ½-inch-thick pieces and fry for 5 minutes on each side until golden brown.

For an even better taste, drizzle with maple syrup, if desired.

Unused portions of the cornmeal mixture can be stored in the refrigerator for several days, and fried as you wish to eat them.

Mom would always make cornmeal mush, but my children aren't so fond of it, so I don't make it too often. Growing up, this was one of the snacks I would have when we came home from school. We would always put apple butter on top of sliced fried mush.

Fried mush is often available in restaurants with Amish foods on the menu.

OVEN OMELET

1 small onion, chopped

2 cups cheddar cheese, shredded (or your favorite cheese)

1 (3-ounce) package chipped beef, cut into small pieces;
 or 1 (2-ounce) package dried beef

8 eggs, beaten

1 cup milk

Salt and pepper, as desired

In a buttered 9 x 13-inch baking pan, layer the onion, cheese, and chipped or dried beef. In a bowl, beat the eggs, milk, and salt and pepper. Carefully pour over ingredients in baking pan.

Bake at 325°F for about 25 minutes, or until eggs are set.

Optional: Cooked bacon pieces, mushrooms, chile peppers, or green bell peppers can be added to the bottom layer.

Recipes are frequently passed around in our family. Some families even make their own cookbooks with all the family favorites. This recipe came from one of my cousins.

POTATO PANCAKES

2 cups potatoes, peeled and grated (drain off any excess liquid)
1 tablespoon onion, finely chopped
1 egg, beaten
2 tablespoons butter, melted
2 tablespoons milk
4 tablespoons flour
1 teaspoon salt
1 teaspoon baking powder
¼ teaspoon black pepper

In a medium bowl, stir all ingredients together. Heat skillet and drop batter by large spoonfuls into skillet, and flatten to make ½-inch pancakes. Brown on one side, then turn and brown on the other, about 5 minutes per side.

You can use nonstick spray or a little butter or oil in the skillet for frying, if needed.

Makes 7 large pancakes.

These potato pancakes are good with a slice of cheese on top, or with bacon crumbled in them before cooking. We have these with biscuits and gravy too sometimes. A tasty recipe!

SAUSAGE GRAVY

2 pounds pork sausage

½ pound butter

2 cups flour

3 quarts (12 cups) milk

1 teaspoon ground pepper

1 tablespoon salt

½ teaspoon dried sage

1 teaspoon garlic powder

1 heaping tablespoon chicken soup base

Place sausage in a large pot and cook over medium heat until thoroughly cooked, stirring and breaking apart while cooking. Drain sausage; reserve. In the same pot, melt butter over medium heat. Add flour and stir constantly until smooth, cooking over medium heat about 5 minutes. Add milk, pepper, salt, sage, garlic powder, and soup base. Continue to cook over medium heat for 10–15 minutes until thickened. Add reserved sausage. If gravy becomes too thick, add a little milk.

Serve over biscuits or toast.

We have sausage gravy often. We have our own sausage and our own milk, so all the ingredients are on hand. Sometimes we even have this for dinner! This is easy to divide in half for a smaller family.

Soups & Salads

BLT SALAD

1 head lettuce, washed and chopped

10 slices bacon, fried and crumbled

4 hard-cooked eggs, chopped

1½ cup tomatoes, seeded and chopped

1 cup cheddar cheese, shredded

2 cups croutons

Dressing

½ cup sugar

1 cup mayonnaise

1 teaspoon prepared mustard

1 tablespoon cider vinegar

1 tablespoon milk

In large bowl, toss all salad ingredients together. In small bowl, mix dressing ingredients together. Pour dressing over salad when ready to serve, tossing well.

This is a very tasty salad, especially when using delicious summer tomatoes. It's handy to have fresh tomatoes in the garden just a few steps out the door.

BROCCOLI SOUP

3 cups chicken broth

5 cups broccoli, chopped

1½ cup onions, chopped

6 tablespoons butter

½ cup flour

3 cups milk

1 teaspoon salt

½ teaspoon pepper

In a 3-quart saucepan, bring broth to a boil. Add broccoli and onions, reduce heat, and simmer until broccoli is tender, about 15 minutes.

In a 5-quart saucepan, melt butter. Add flour and stir until smooth, about 5 minutes. Add milk slowly, whisking to combine. Add salt and pepper. Cook over medium heat until thick, about 10 minutes. Add 1 cup of the broccoli stock to milk mixture; stir until blended. Gradually add the rest of the broccoli stock. Cook together for a few minutes until well blended.

Broccoli was never something I would eat as a child, but with age you learn to like more foods. The children love a bowl of warm soup after coming in from doing the chores in the barn.

CABBAGE SALAD

1 gallon cabbage, shredded (about 16 cups, or 2 medium heads cabbage)
1 tablespoon salt
1 cup carrot, shredded
1 medium onion, diced (use red onion for extra color)
1 cup green bell pepper, chopped
1 cup celery, chopped
1½ cup sugar
¾ cup white vinegar
¾ cup vegetable oil

Put shredded cabbage in a dish or pan and spread out to about 1½ inch thick. Sprinkle salt all over surface of cabbage. Let stand, without stirring, for 1 hour. After 1 hour, add the carrot, onion, bell pepper, and celery, mixing well.

In a medium saucepan, bring sugar, vinegar, and oil to a boil. Remove from heat and immediately pour over cabbage mixture. Do not stir. Refrigerate until cold; this will take several hours.

Once salad is cold, stir well and store in covered containers. I prefer large glass jars, but plastic will work fine. Stays very crisp in refrigerator for several days.

We grow our own cabbage in the garden. The cabbage keeps for a long time in our refrigerator in the basement.

CHILI SOUP

2 pounds sausage (may substitute ground beef or venison)
1 fresh garlic clove, minced; or 1 teaspoon garlic powder
1 medium onion, diced
1 green bell pepper, diced
1 (15-ounce) can kidney beans, undrained
3–4 cups tomato juice
1 tablespoon chili powder
¼ cup brown sugar
Salt and pepper, to taste

Brown sausage, garlic, onion, and bell pepper. Drain, then combine in a saucepan along with remaining ingredients. Bring to a boil, then reduce heat to low and simmer for a while, 30–60 minutes for best flavor.

My mother used to use ground beef or sausage to make her chili soup, but we enjoy the taste of sausage more. Sometimes in the summer if I have jalapeño peppers, I'll use them instead of chili powder, simmering one with the soup and then removing it before serving.

CREAM OF MUSHROOM SOUP

3 cups fresh mushrooms, chopped
1 small onion, chopped
2 cups chicken broth
3 tablespoons butter
3 tablespoons flour
1½ cup milk
½ cup cream
Salt and pepper, to taste

In a large saucepan, combine the mushrooms, onion, and broth, and heat over high heat for 1 minute. Reduce heat to low, bring to a simmer, and simmer, covered, for 15 minutes.

Melt the butter in a small saucepan, and stir in the flour to make a paste. Add the flour paste to the mushroom mixture; stir. Increase the heat to medium and slowly add the milk, stirring constantly. When the mixture thickens and begins to boil, stir in the cream.

Turn down to medium heat and cook until mushrooms are tender. Season with salt and pepper.

I use cream of mushroom soup in many of my casseroles, and I use it on my pot roast. I would have this for lunch often when the children were little.

DANDELION SOUR CREAM SALAD

½ cup mayonnaise
1 cup cider vinegar
2½ cups whole milk
Salt, to taste
4 cups young dandelion greens, packed
4 hard-cooked eggs, peeled and chopped

Combine the mayonnaise, cider vinegar, milk, and salt in a jar with a lid or another sealed container. Shake until thoroughly blended.

Put dandelion greens and eggs in a large bowl. Pour dressing over top and toss.

We only have dandelion greens in the early spring weeks. Once the yellow flowers pop up, the greens will taste too bitter to use. We like putting this salad over steamed potatoes. Fried bacon along with this is even better!

HOMEMADE CUCUMBER SALAD (FOR CANNING)

25–30 medium-sized cucumbers, peeled and thinly sliced

8 large white onions, chopped

2 large green bell peppers, chopped

½ cup salt

5 cups white vinegar

5 cups sugar

1 teaspoon ground turmeric

½ teaspoon ground cloves

2 tablespoons mustard seed

In a large bowl, combine the cucumbers, onions, bell peppers, and salt. Allow to stand for 3 hours, then drain off liquid.

In a very large pot, combine the vinegar, sugar, turmeric, cloves, and mustard seed, and bring to a rapid boil. Add the drained vegetables and stir until they are evenly coated. Continue cooking over medium heat until the mixture starts to simmer.

This salad may be refrigerated or canned. To can, ladle into hot pint jars, leaving ¼-inch headspace. Wipe jar rims with a dampened paper towel. Adjust lids and process in a boiling-water canner for 15 minutes.

Makes 8–10 pint jars.

Note: Canning times are subject to change according to USDA regulations. For the latest canning times, check your county extension office or the National Center for Home Food Preservation website.

This is a pickle-type cucumber and is good with sandwiches. My mother would always serve these at church lunch.

LOADED POTATO SOUP

1 pound bacon, fried and chopped

2 celery ribs, diced

1 onion, diced

6–8 potatoes, peeled and cubed

4 cups chicken broth

3 tablespoons butter

¼ cup flour

1 cup heavy cream

2 cups cheddar cheese, shredded

Salt and pepper, to taste

Place fried bacon in a large pot. Add celery and onion and cook until softened. (Use bacon grease, if desired.) Add potatoes and chicken broth. Bring to a boil, then reduce heat and simmer until potatoes are tender.

In a small saucepan, melt butter, then whisk in flour and cook for a few minutes, stirring constantly, until the mixture is browned. Slowly add heavy cream, whisking constantly. Bring to a boil, then reduce heat and continue whisking until mixture thickens. Stir cream mixture into the potato mixture. Gently stir in cheese. Add salt and pepper.

Serves 12 or more.

This is quite different from the Simple Potato Soup (page 78) my mom made when I was young. This is a thick, hearty soup that when served with a good bread would be a meal in itself.

AMISH MACARONI SALAD

3 cups cooked macaroni
½ cup carrots, chopped
½ cup celery, chopped
½ cup onion, chopped
2 tablespoons prepared mustard
1 cup whipped salad dressing
2 tablespoons cider vinegar
½ teaspoon salt
½ cup sugar
2 tablespoons milk
Salt and pepper, to taste

Mix macaroni, carrots, celery, and onion in a big bowl until evenly combined. In a separate bowl, mix mustard, whipped salad dressing, vinegar, salt, sugar, milk, and salt and pepper. Combine with macaroni mixture and toss until thoroughly mixed. Refrigerate and serve.

This is one of my husband, Joe's, favorite salads. I like to add chopped hard-cooked eggs sometimes. We usually have plenty of eggs, as we have our own laying hens.

MOM'S (ELIZABETH COBLENTZ) SIMPLE POTATO SOUP

3 cups potatoes, peeled and diced
¾ cup onion, chopped
4 cups milk
¼ cup butter
Salt and pepper, to taste

Put potatoes and onion in pot and add water until just covered. Cook until tender, 25–30 minutes. Mash potatoes and onions with a potato masher right in the water you cooked them in.

Add the milk, butter, and salt and pepper. Heat until hot, but do not boil.

This is how my mom made potato soup when I was growing up, and now I make it too. It's very simple but has a lot of flavor. When unexpected company would show up, my mom would add more milk to the soup to make it go further.

PASTA SALAD

12 ounces angel hair pasta

¾ cup pepperoni

½ cup tomatoes, diced

½ cup green or red bell peppers, chopped

1 whole cucumber, chopped

½ cup red onions, chopped

1 (2¼-ounce) can sliced black olives, drained

Dressing

¼ cup oil

½ cup cider vinegar

¾ cup sugar

½ teaspoon salt

½ teaspoon dried oregano

½ teaspoon Italian seasoning

Sprinkle garlic powder

Cook pasta according to package directions; drain and cool. Add pepperoni and vegetables. In a small bowl, whisk dressing ingredients together; pour over salad.

Refrigerate at least 1 hour before serving. Can be made a day ahead.

This is a very good salad to take to a family reunion or potluck dinner.

PEA AND CHEESE SALAD

1 (12-ounce) package frozen peas, thawed, or an equivalent amount fresh peas,
   cooked until just tender
1 cup celery, chopped
2 hard-cooked eggs, chopped
1 cup Colby cheese, cubed
½ cup radishes, sliced
¼ cup green onion, chopped
1 cup mayonnaise
1 tablespoon prepared mustard
2 tablespoons sugar
1 teaspoon seasoned salt

If using fresh peas, cook until just tender; drain. If using frozen peas, let them thaw slightly but no need to cook.

In a medium bowl, combine the peas, celery, eggs, cheese, radishes, and green onion. In a small bowl, stir together the mayonnaise, mustard, sugar, and salt. Pour mayonnaise mixture over the vegetable mixture and mix well. Refrigerate until ready to serve.

If you like peas, I'm sure you will like this salad. Some of our children like to eat peas right from the pod but won't touch them after they are cooked.

POTATO SALAD

2½ pounds potatoes, peeled and cooked (whole) until tender
6 hard-cooked eggs, chopped
1 cup celery, chopped
1 small onion, chopped
1½ cup whipped salad dressing or mayonnaise
2 teaspoons prepared mustard
¼ cup cider vinegar
¼ cup milk
¾ cup sugar
2 teaspoons salt

Dice cooked potatoes or put through a slicer. Combine potatoes, eggs, celery, and onion in a large bowl. In a medium bowl, whisk together the whipped salad dressing or mayonnaise, mustard, vinegar, milk, sugar, and salt. Pour over potato mixture and stir together.

Can be served immediately, but is better if refrigerated for a few hours.

Potato salad is popular in the Amish community. It can be served at weddings, funerals, reunions, and picnics. At home we would eat potato salad on bread for sandwiches.

SAUERKRAUT SALAD

3 cups sauerkraut, drained and rinsed
½ cup onion, chopped
½ cup celery, chopped
1 green bell pepper, chopped
1½ cup sugar
1½ cup water
½ cup cider vinegar

In a bowl, combine sauerkraut, onion, celery, and bell pepper. In a saucepan, combine sugar, water, and vinegar. Bring to a boil, stirring occasionally. Let cool, then add liquid to vegetable mixture and stir well.

Let stand in refrigerator overnight or 8–12 hours before serving.

I think I'm the only one in our family who eats sauerkraut. I like it best with brats (bratwurst).

SWEET AND SOUR DRESSING

¾ cup white vinegar
1½ cup vegetable oil
¾ cup mayonnaise or whipped salad dressing
¼ cup prepared yellow mustard
2½ cups sugar
1½ teaspoon celery seed
1½ teaspoon pepper
1½ teaspoon onion salt

Whisk or shake together all ingredients until well blended. Keeps well in refrigerator.

Makes 1 quart.

A very good dressing if you like to make your own.

SPINACH SALAD

10 ounces fresh spinach, torn into pieces
1 pound fresh mushrooms, sliced
½ pound bacon, cooked and crumbled
3 celery ribs, chopped
1 cup cheddar cheese, shredded
3 hard-cooked eggs, chopped
3 green onions, sliced

Dressing
1 cup ketchup
¾ cup vegetable oil
¾ cup white vinegar
1 teaspoon Worcestershire sauce
½ cup sugar
1 teaspoon salt

In a large bowl, combine the spinach, mushrooms, bacon, celery, cheese, eggs, and green onions.

In another bowl, whisk together dressing ingredients until sugar is dissolved. Drizzle the amount of dressing you prefer over salad; toss. Serve immediately.

If you have extra dressing, it can be stored in refrigerator for up to 2 weeks.

If you are looking for a change in salads, try this. I used to dislike the taste of spinach, but now that I'm older I have learned to like it.

STAY-CRISP COLESLAW

1 medium head cabbage, shredded

2 carrots, shredded

1 green bell pepper, chopped

¼ cup onion, chopped

¾ cup cold water, divided

1 (¼-ounce) envelope unflavored gelatin

⅔ cup white vinegar

⅔ cup sugar

1 teaspoon celery seed

1½ teaspoon salt

Black pepper, to taste

⅔ cup vegetable oil

Mix together cabbage, carrots, bell pepper, and onion. Sprinkle with ½ cup cold water. Cover and refrigerate until crisp, about 1 hour. Soften gelatin in ¼ cup additional cold water.

In a saucepan, combine vinegar, sugar, celery seed, salt, and black pepper and bring to a boil. Stir in gelatin mixture. Cool until dressing is slightly thickened. Beat well and gradually stir in vegetable oil.

Drain refrigerated vegetables. Pour dressing over top and toss until cabbage is well coated. Refrigerate until serving time. This coleslaw stays crisp for several days in refrigerator.

I always like to plant a few different varieties of cabbage. I like to plant an early and a late kind of cabbage plant so I have plenty of cabbage all season long.

VEGETABLE SOUP

1 pint canned beef chunks or any raw beef roast or stew meat, cut into small
   pieces
1 medium yellow onion, cleaned but whole, stem removed
2 potatoes, peeled and diced
1 cup carrots, diced
1 cup green beans, diced
2 cups corn kernels
2 cups peas
4 cups tomato juice
1½ teaspoon salt
1½ teaspoon ground pepper

Brown the beef in a large skillet over medium heat. Put the beef and the
whole onion in a large pot and add the remaining ingredients. Add enough
water to cover the vegetables. Cook over medium heat for 45–50 minutes
until the vegetables are soft. Remove onion and serve.

*Our children always called this Grandma's soup. My mother would make
it a lot and they really loved it. It is an easy soup to make. I like to make
a big batch of it, then put it in quart jars and process it. On busy days
you can just open a few jars and heat it up and have a quick meal. Our
family likes to eat Colby cheese and saltine crackers with this soup. It is
also easy to put in lunches for school or work.*

Vegetables & Sides

There are not as many dishes in this chapter as in the other chapters. This is largely because we mostly cook vegetables very simply, by lightly boiling or steaming, or perhaps browning them in a pan or the oven. We especially love vegetables fresh out of the garden, or out of jars that we have home-canned, or frozen and stored in the freezer. Our freezer is powered by gas, not electricity.

ASPARAGUS EGG CASSEROLE

2 pounds fresh asparagus, rinsed and cut into 1- to 1½-inch pieces
4 hard-cooked eggs, sliced
10 saltine crackers, crumbled, or bread crumbs

White sauce
4 tablespoons butter
4 tablespoons flour
1 cup milk
1 cup reserved asparagus water (see instructions)
1 teaspoon salt
½ teaspoon garlic powder
¼ teaspoon black pepper
1½ cup cheddar cheese, shredded

Bring a medium pot of water to a boil. Add cut asparagus and boil for 5 minutes, or until asparagus is crisp-tender. Drain asparagus, reserving 1 cup liquid. Rinse asparagus under cold water to stop the cooking process.

In a saucepan over medium heat, melt the butter. Whisk in the flour and stir continuously to make a roux (thick base for sauce), about 1 minute. Add the milk, reserved asparagus water, salt, garlic powder, and black pepper. Cook, stirring constantly, until thick, about 10 minutes. Add cheese and stir until melted.

In a 9 x 13-inch baking dish, layer the cooked asparagus, sliced eggs, and cheese sauce. Top with the crumbled crackers or bread crumbs. Bake at 350°F for 20–25 minutes, or until lightly browned and bubbly on edges.

When we moved to Michigan, the property had a large asparagus patch. We were disappointed that much of it was lost when we built our house. We replanted, and each year the patch gets a little bigger.

AMISH DRESSING

1 tablespoon chicken soup base

2 cups hot water

½ cup carrot, diced

½ cup celery, chopped

½ cup yellow onion, chopped

4 large eggs, beaten

20 slices bread, crumbled (day-old works well)

1 teaspoon seasoned salt

Dissolve the soup base in the hot water. Add all the remaining ingredients and mix well. If it is too dry, add more water.

Pour into buttered two quart baking dish and bake, uncovered, at 350°F for 45 minutes.

We have dressing a lot of times when we serve mashed potatoes and gravy. We like putting gravy over our dressing too. I've also included a large quantity recipe for dressing in the Amish Weddings section of this cookbook.

FRESH SQUASH CASSEROLE

3 cups zucchini or yellow squash, sliced or chopped

¼ cup onion, chopped

4 tablespoons butter or margarine

2 eggs, beaten

¼ cup milk

½ teaspoon salt

½ teaspoon pepper

1 cup sharp cheddar cheese, shredded

1 cup buttery crackers, crushed

Sauté squash and onion in butter or margarine until tender, then drain. In a bowl, mix squash-onion mixture with eggs, milk, salt, and pepper. Spoon into a greased 9 x 13-inch baking pan. Top with cheese and crackers. Bake at 350°F for 20 minutes.

This is an easy casserole to make when you have plenty of squash in the summer months.

STUFFED PEPPERS

6 green bell peppers

1 pound ground beef

2 tablespoons onion, chopped

1 teaspoon salt, divided

Pepper, as desired

⅛ teaspoon garlic salt

1 cup cooked white rice

1 (15-ounce) can tomato sauce, divided

¾ cup mozzarella cheese, shredded

Bring a large pot of water with ½ teaspoon salt to a boil. Cut the tops off the bell peppers and remove the seeds. Cook peppers in boiling water for 5 minutes, then drain. Sprinkle a few grains of salt in each pepper.

In a large skillet, sauté beef and onions for 5 minutes, or until beef is browned. Drain off excess fat, and season with ½ teaspoon salt and desired pepper. Stir in garlic salt, cooked rice, and 1 cup tomato sauce. Stuff each pepper with the beef-and-rice mixture, and place stuffed peppers open end up in a baking dish. Pour remaining tomato sauce over the peppers.

Cover and cook at 350°F for 45 minutes. Uncover, sprinkle with cheese, and cook for an additional 15 minutes.

I've been told that if you want a good green bell pepper for cooking, pick one that has three bumps on the bottom. If you want a sweeter green bell pepper, choose one that has four bumps on the bottom.

SWEET POTATO CASSEROLE

3 medium sweet potatoes; or 3 cups sweet potatoes, cooked and mashed

½ cup granulated sugar

½ cup butter, softened

2 eggs, beaten

½ cup milk

1 tablespoon vanilla extract

Topping

½ cup butter, melted

½ cup flour

1 cup brown sugar, packed

½ cup nuts, chopped

If using fresh sweet potatoes, peel and cut into large chunks. Place in medium saucepan and cover with water. Bring to a boil and cook for about 15 minutes, or until tender. Drain the sweet potatoes well, and mash with potato masher or fork.

In a bowl, mix the mashed sweet potatoes, granulated sugar, butter, eggs, milk, and vanilla. Place in a greased 2-quart baking dish.

In a small bowl, combine the topping ingredients. Sprinkle over sweet potato mixture.

Bake at 350°F for 25–30 minutes, or until sides begin to bubble.

If you enjoy sweet potatoes, I'm sure you will enjoy this casserole!

ZUCCHINI FRITTERS

2 medium zucchini, grated

1 teaspoon salt

2 tablespoons onion, finely chopped

1 carrot, grated

2 tablespoons fresh parsley, finely chopped

1 egg, beaten

½ cup flour

Dash pepper

Oil, for frying

Mix zucchini and salt; let stand in strainer over bowl or sink for 15 minutes. Squeeze out excess liquid. In a bowl, stir together the salted zucchini and onion, carrot, parsley, egg, flour, and pepper.

In a skillet, heat oil over medium-high heat. Drop zucchini mixture by tablespoonfuls into pan and fry for 5 minutes on each side, or until golden brown. Place cooked fritters on paper towels to remove excess grease.

This is a well-loved recipe in our family. I sometimes substitute zucchini in some casserole dishes that call for potatoes.

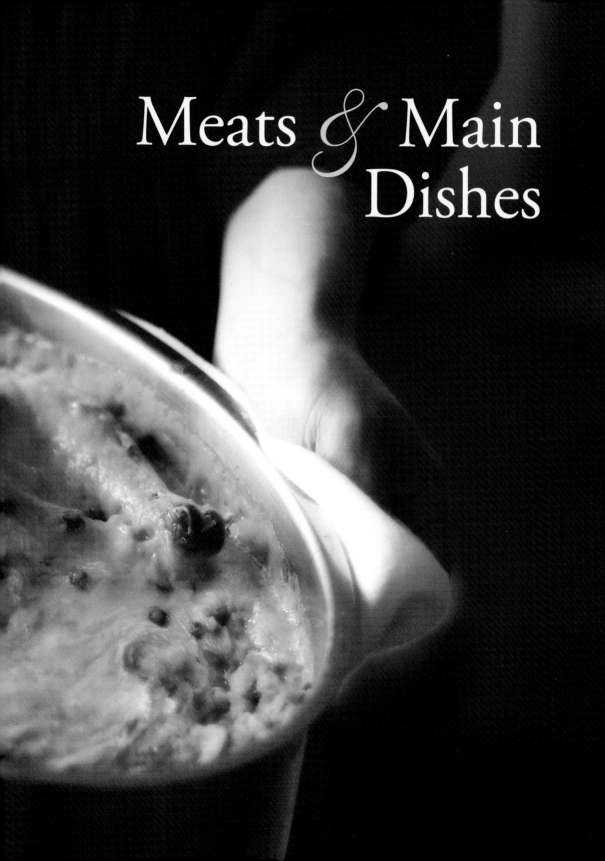

Meats & Main Dishes

BARBECUED MEATBALLS

Meatballs

3 pounds ground beef

2 cups oats

1 cup onion, chopped

1¾ cup milk

2 eggs

½ teaspoon garlic powder

½ teaspoon black pepper

2 teaspoons salt

2 teaspoons chili powder

Sauce

2 cups ketchup

1 tablespoon liquid smoke

½ cup onion, chopped

1½ cup brown sugar, packed

½ teaspoon garlic powder

1 tablespoon prepared mustard

Combine all meatball ingredients in large bowl, mixing well with large spoon or your hands. Shape into meatballs and place in 9 x 13-inch baking pan (you may need an additional baking pan to fit all the meatballs) and bake at 350°F for about 30 minutes. Carefully drain excess grease.

In a medium bowl, combine all the sauce ingredients. Pour over meatballs and bake an additional 45–60 minutes at 350°F.

My family enjoys these served with mashed potatoes or noodles. They taste good as leftovers too, if there are any!

BBQ CHICKEN SANDWICHES

2 cups celery, diced

1 cup onion, diced

1 cup green bell pepper, diced

1 teaspoon salt

1 teaspoon pepper

4 tablespoons butter

6 cups chicken, cooked and diced

¼ cup brown sugar, packed

2 cups ketchup

2 teaspoons prepared mustard

2 cups water

1 tablespoon Worcestershire sauce

Salt and pepper, to taste

In a Dutch oven or large pan, sauté celery, onion, bell pepper, salt, and pepper in butter until tender, about 5 minutes. Add the remaining ingredients and simmer over low heat for 1 hour, stirring occasionally. Serve on buns.

Makes 15 good-sized sandwiches.

We raise our own layer chickens for eggs, and when they get older we butcher them and can the meat and broth. We also get butchering chickens (broilers) every year that are usually big enough to butcher for meat by four to six weeks old. This meat we put in the freezer to grill or fry.

At one time, we didn't raise our own chickens; I would buy my meat in a store. So the first time we butchered, our oldest daughter, Elizabeth, didn't want to eat chicken for a long time after that. But for the most part, it wasn't a problem for the children to know where the meat came from. Our youngest son, Kevin, doesn't like roosters anyway (they can be mean and give people trouble), so he laughs that the rooster will become our dinner.

CAMPFIRE STEW

2 cups beef stew meat (may substitute a roast, cut into chunks)

4 cups red potatoes, unpeeled, cleaned, and diced

2 cups green beans, cut into small pieces

1 whole onion (used to flavor the soup; it is removed before eating)

4–5 beef bouillon cubes

1 teaspoon garlic powder

Salt and pepper, to taste

Put beef chunks in kettle (or large pot) with enough water to cover, bring to a boil, and boil for 10 minutes. Add potatoes, green beans, and onion, adding enough water so that vegetables are well covered. Add bouillon. Boil until vegetables and meat are tender. Season with garlic powder and salt and pepper. Remove onion if you wish.

Our family makes this often in a kettle outside over a fire. I like to get the green beans, potatoes, and onions right out of my garden. It is more like a soup than a stew, but this is what we have always called it.

CHICKEN SQUASH CASSEROLE

6 cups zucchini, unpeeled and sliced

1½ cup onion, chopped

½ cup green bell pepper, chopped

4 cups chicken, cooked and diced

1 (10¾-ounce) can cream of mushroom soup

1 (10¾-ounce) can cream of chicken soup

½ cup sour cream

½ teaspoon garlic powder

½ teaspoon black pepper

2 cups cheddar cheese, shredded

4 tablespoons butter, melted

1 cup bread crumbs

Put zucchini, onions, and bell pepper in a large skillet. Add enough water to a depth of halfway up the vegetables. Bring to a boil over high heat. Turn down to medium-high heat; cover. Cook until vegetables are tender but not mushy, about 10 minutes. Pour into strainer and drain well.

In a bowl, mix the well-drained vegetables, chicken, soups, sour cream, garlic powder, and pepper. Place mixture in a 9 x 13-inch baking pan that has been buttered or coated with nonstick spray. Cover mixture with cheese. Toss melted butter with bread crumbs, then sprinkle on top of cheese.

Bake, uncovered, at 350°F for 30–45 minutes, or until bubbly on edges.

The first year I had a garden, I planted twelve zucchini plants. I had more zucchini than I knew what to do with! The next year I planted two plants and they both died, so I didn't have any zucchini that year. So goes life with zucchini.

DEEP DISH PIZZA

Crust

2¼ cups flour

1 tablespoon baking powder

¼ teaspoon salt

1 cup milk

¼ cup butter, at room temperature

Filling

1 pound ground beef, cooked and drained

½ cup olives (black or green), sliced

¼ cup onion, chopped

2 (4-ounce) cans sliced mushrooms, drained

1 (6-ounce) can tomato paste

1 teaspoon salt

½ teaspoon dried oregano

¼ teaspoon garlic powder

1½ cup mozzarella cheese, shredded

In a large bowl, stir together all the crust ingredients until a ball of dough forms. If you have a mixer, use the dough hook and mix on low until dough forms a ball. Sprinkle flour onto a rolling pin and your hands. Place dough on slightly floured surface and roll into rectangle to fit a 9 x 13-inch baking pan. If dough is too sticky, pat with a little more flour. Grease the baking pan with oil and place dough in pan, pushing dough to edges.

In a large bowl, combine all filling ingredients except the cheese. Spoon filling onto crust. Bake at 425°F for 18–20 minutes. Sprinkle cheese on top and return to oven until cheese is melted and lightly browned, 5–10 minutes.

Cool 5 minutes before serving.

My husband, Joe's, favorite part of this pizza is the olives. My son Kevin picks his off and gives them to his dad. Italian sausage can be substituted for ground beef.

HOBO SUPPERS

10 red potatoes, unpeeled and cut into chunks

½ cup onion, diced

½ cup green bell pepper, diced

2 cups carrots, sliced

1 cup celery, chopped

1 (16-ounce) package smoky links, cut into pieces; or 1 pound smoked sausage, cut into pieces

Salt and pepper, as desired

Cheese, sliced

Preheat grill to medium-high heat.

In a bowl, mix all the ingredients together except the cheese. Divide the mixture into the amount you want for each serving, placing individual servings on sheets of aluminum foil. Fold foil over, wrapping tight, and set on grill for 10 minutes on each side.

Open up foil; if potatoes are soft, add a slice of cheese. (If potatoes need more time to cook, close pouches and return to grill before adding cheese.) Re-wrap and grill a few more minutes until cheese is melted.

Alternatively, can be cooked in oven at 400°F for 10 minutes, then turned over and cooked for 10 additional minutes. Check doneness of potatoes before adding cheese.

Hobo Suppers make a great dinner when it's hot outside and I don't want to heat up the kitchen. I gather the onions and green bell peppers right out of my garden and we head to the grill. The children help assemble these suppers wrapped in foil.

HOMESTYLE POT ROAST

3–4 pounds boneless beef pot roast
6–8 small red potatoes, halved or quartered
2 medium onions, quartered
1 pound carrots, peeled and cut into 2-inch pieces
2 (10¾-ounce) cans cream of mushroom soup

Place roast, potatoes, onions, and carrots in a roaster. Spread cream of mushroom soup over everything. Bake, covered, at 325°F for 2½–3 hours, or until roast is tender.

When I make this recipe, I cut the roast into chunks before the roast is cooked, which seems to save on baking time.

JUICY MEAT LOAF

1½ pound ground beef

¾ cup rolled oats

1 cup onion, chopped

2 eggs, beaten

1 cup tomato juice

2 teaspoons salt

¼ teaspoon pepper

¼ cup ketchup

2 tablespoons prepared yellow mustard

3 tablespoons brown sugar

Preheat oven to 350°F. In large bowl, thoroughly mix the ground beef, oats, onion, eggs, tomato juice, salt, and pepper. Pack firmly into 9 x 5-inch loaf pan coated with nonstick cooking spray.

In a small bowl, whisk together ketchup, mustard, and brown sugar. Spread on top of meat loaf.

Bake for 1 hour. Remove from oven and let stand for 5–10 minutes before serving.

I like to serve this with baked beans and scalloped potatoes. Each dish can cook in the oven at the same time for a good Sunday lunch.

Do you want to talk to the man in charge or the woman who knows what's going on?

LAZY DAY LASAGNA

1 (16-ounce) container cottage cheese

3 cups mozzarella cheese, shredded and divided

2 eggs

⅓ cup fresh parsley, chopped

1 teaspoon onion powder

½ teaspoon dried basil

⅛ teaspoon ground pepper

1 (45-ounce) jar spaghetti sauce

1 pound ground beef, cooked and drained (may substitute Italian sausage)

12 lasagna noodles, uncooked

Parmesan cheese, grated, for topping

In a large bowl, mix cottage cheese, 2½ cups mozzarella cheese, eggs, parsley, onion powder, basil, and pepper. In another bowl, mix spaghetti sauce and cooked ground beef.

In a 9 x 13-inch baking dish, spread ¾ cup meat sauce. Lay three uncooked noodles on top. Spread one-third of the cheese mixture and an additional 1¼ cup meat sauce. Repeat layers two times. Top with remaining 3 uncooked noodles and remaining meat sauce. Pour 1 cup water around edges of dish.

Cover tightly with aluminum foil. Bake at 375°F for 45 minutes. Uncover, add remaining ½ cup mozzarella cheese, and bake 15 minutes more, or until noodles are tender. Let stand 10 minutes before serving.

Serve with grated Parmesan cheese. Can be assembled a day ahead and refrigerated until ready to bake.

I like to bring this to a potluck or when I need to bring a meal to someone, like the new moms in church, or if someone is under the weather.

OVEN CRUSTY CHICKEN

1 (2½- to 3-pound) frying chicken, cut into pieces
4 cups crispy rice cereal
½–⅔ cup butter, melted
1 teaspoon salt
¼ teaspoon pepper

Rinse chicken pieces and dry thoroughly. Pour cereal into a gallon-sized resealable plastic bag and crush slightly with rolling pin. Pour into a large bowl. In a medium bowl, combine melted butter with salt and pepper.

Dip chicken pieces, one at a time, into seasoned butter, then roll in cereal until well coated. Place skin side up in a shallow baking dish that has been lined with aluminum foil. Do not crowd pieces.

Bake at 350°F for 1 hour, or until chicken is tender. Do not cover pan or turn pieces while baking.

When I am busy and don't have time to fry my chicken, this is an easy way to have a good crunchy crust on chicken.

PIZZA CASSEROLE

1 pound sausage
⅓ cup onions, chopped
½ cup green bell peppers, diced
1 (4-ounce) can sliced mushrooms, drained
½ teaspoon salt
8 ounces rotini pasta, cooked
2 (10-ounce) cans pizza sauce, or equivalent amount homemade sauce
2 cups mozzarella cheese, shredded
15–18 slices pepperoni (optional)

Brown the sausage, onion, and bell peppers in a skillet. Drain grease. Add the mushrooms and salt, then spoon into a greased 9 x 13-inch baking dish. Cover with cooked rotini. Pour sauce over top and sprinkle with cheese. If desired, arrange pepperoni on top of the cheese.

Bake at 350°F for 30 minutes, or until cheese has melted and casserole is bubbling.

Note: This recipe can be made a day ahead; add 15 minutes to baking time if casserole has been refrigerated.

Our family always enjoys pizza casserole. With our own sausage on hand, this recipe is convenient. We never have leftovers when I fix this. I like making it for potlucks or evenings after church services.

OVERNIGHT TURKEY CASSEROLE

2 cups cooked turkey, chopped

½ cup celery, diced

½ cup green bell pepper, diced

½ cup onion, diced

½ cup mayonnaise

½ teaspoon salt

¼ teaspoon pepper

6 slices bread, cubed

1½ cup milk

3 eggs

1 (10¾-ounce) can cream of mushroom soup

1 cup cheddar cheese, shredded

In a bowl, combine turkey, celery, bell pepper, onion, mayonnaise, salt, and pepper.

Place half the bread cubes in a large greased baking dish or 9 x 13-inch baking pan. Pour turkey mixture over top and add the remaining bread cubes.

In a bowl, mix the milk, eggs, and soup and pour over top of casserole. Let stand in refrigerator overnight, or 8–12 hours. Top with cheese and bake, uncovered, at 350°F for 1 hour.

This is a good casserole to use up leftover turkey. It is supposed to be made the day before you bake it, but if you make it in the morning it will work well also.

VENISON BAKE

⅓ cup onion, finely chopped

⅓ cup green bell pepper, chopped

2 tablespoons butter or margarine

1 pound ground venison

1 egg

½ cup milk

⅓ cup ketchup

1 teaspoon Worcestershire sauce

½ teaspoon prepared mustard

15 saltine crackers, crushed

½ teaspoon salt

¼ teaspoon pepper

Sauté onion and bell pepper in butter or margarine for about 5 minutes. In a large bowl, thoroughly mix sautéed vegetables with the venison, egg, milk, ketchup, Worcestershire sauce, mustard, crackers, salt, and pepper. Put in a 9 x 5-inch loaf pan and bake at 350°F for 1 hour.

My husband, Joe, and the boys enjoy hunting for deer. The three boys were excited to pass their hunter safety course! In our area, once kids get old enough to hunt, they are required to pass a safety course consisting of about fifty questions! Kevin was so proud when he passed his.

WHOLE BAKED CHICKEN

1 (2–3 pound) whole chicken, ready for roasting (insides removed)
1 (10¾-ounce) can cream of mushroom soup
½ cup milk
1 cup cheddar cheese, shredded and divided
Salt and pepper, as desired

Preheat the oven to 350°F. Rinse and clean chicken; pat to dry. Place chicken in a 2-quart baking dish or small roasting pan. In a medium bowl, combine soup, milk, and ½ cup cheese. Stir to blend. Pour mixture over chicken and season with salt and pepper.

Cover and bake for 1 hour. Sprinkle the remaining ½ cup cheese on top. Bake until cheese is melted, about 15 minutes longer.

When we raise our chickens for butchering, we only have them for five to six weeks and then they are ready to butcher. I like to leave some chickens whole for recipes like this.

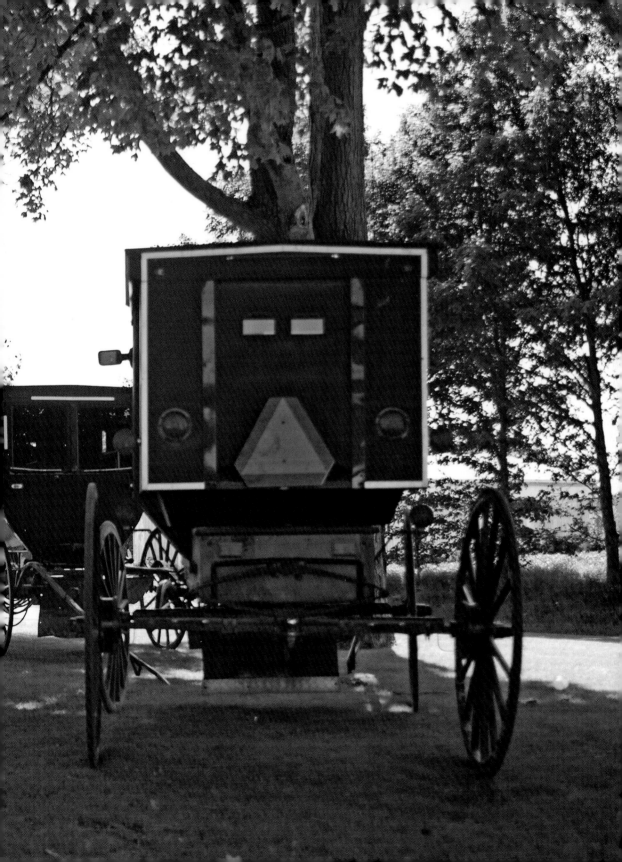

Cakes & Frostings

BLUEBERRY SNACK CAKE

2 cups all-purpose flour

1½ cup sugar

½ cup cold butter or margarine, cubed

1 teaspoon baking powder

1 cup milk

2 eggs, separated

2 cups fresh or frozen blueberries

In a mixing bowl, combine flour and sugar. Cut in butter or margarine until crumbly. Reserve ¾ cup of this mixture for topping. To the remaining mixture, add the baking powder, milk, and egg yolks, mixing well. In a separate bowl, beat egg whites until soft peaks form, then fold into batter.

Pour into a greased 9 x 13-inch pan. Sprinkle with blueberries and reserved crumb mixture. (If using frozen blueberries, do not thaw before adding to the batter.)

Bake at 350°F for 30–35 minutes, or until golden brown.

I didn't used to bake much with blueberries because they aren't my favorite, but when a friend dropped by with some fresh blueberries a few years back, I was surprised to find out our children really liked them. Now I bake with them more often, especially when they are in season. I'm told they add healthy nutrition, so that's great!

BUTTERMILK SPICE CAKE

2 cups sugar
½ cup butter
2 cups buttermilk
3½ cups flour
2 teaspoons baking soda
1 teaspoon ground cinnamon
½ teaspoon ground nutmeg
¼ teaspoon ground allspice

Cream together sugar and butter. Add buttermilk, flour, baking soda, cinnamon, nutmeg, and allspice. Mix until well combined.

Pour batter into a greased and floured 9 x 13-inch baking pan. Bake at 350°F for 30–35 minutes, or until a toothpick inserted in the middle comes out clean.

Tastes good plain or with powdered sugar sifted on top.

I always have plenty of buttermilk on hand to make this cake. After I make my butter from the milk from our cows, the liquid that is left is buttermilk. If you don't have buttermilk on hand, you can make your own by putting 1 tablespoon vinegar in a 1-cup measuring device. Fill to the 1-cup line with milk. Let stand about 5 minutes, and then you have a buttermilk or sour milk substitute.

CARROT CAKE

4 eggs
2 cups sugar
1 cup vegetable oil
2 cups flour
1 teaspoon ground cinnamon
2 teaspoons baking soda
1 teaspoon salt
3 cups carrots, peeled and grated
½ cup nuts, chopped

With an electric mixer, beat eggs, sugar, and oil at medium speed until smooth. In a separate bowl, sift together flour, cinnamon, baking soda, and salt. Add egg mixture, beating at low speed until blended. Fold carrots and nuts into batter and stir until well blended.

Pour into a greased and floured 9 x 13-inch baking pan. Bake at 350°F for 35–40 minutes, or until a toothpick inserted in center of cake comes out clean. Cool.

Frosting
4 ounces cream cheese
¼ cup butter, at room temperature
2½ cups powdered sugar
1 teaspoon ground cinnamon
2 tablespoons milk
1 teaspoon vanilla extract

In a small bowl, mix cream cheese and butter until well blended. Add remaining ingredients and mix well. Spread over cooled cake.

When I grow carrots in my garden, I don't dig them all up right away. I leave them in the ground well into the fall and early winter, and cover them with straw or leaves. When I need some, I go and dig up what I need.

CARAMEL FROSTING

¼ cup butter
1½ cup brown sugar, firmly packed
¼ teaspoon salt
¼ cup milk
2¼ cups powdered sugar
1 teaspoon vanilla extract

Melt butter in a saucepan. Stir in brown sugar and salt. Cook on low heat, stirring constantly, for 2 minutes. Add milk. Increase heat, continue stirring, and bring to a boil. Remove from heat and let cool a little. Whisk in powdered sugar and vanilla. Spread on cake or sweet rolls.

This frosting can be used on cakes or cinnamon rolls. It's a nice change from vanilla frosting and goes well on any chocolate cake, or brownies.

COOKIE DOUGH FROSTING FOR BROWNIES

½ cup butter or margarine, softened

½ cup brown sugar, packed

¼ cup granulated sugar

1 cup flour

3 tablespoons milk

1 teaspoon vanilla extract

1 cup chocolate chips

Mix all ingredients together and spread on top of your favorite brownies.

This is a good way to top off plain brownies. Our children enjoy this for a change once in a while.

CREAM CHEESE ICING

¼ cup butter or margarine, softened

8 ounces cream cheese, softened

3 cups powdered sugar

1 teaspoon vanilla extract

2–4 teaspoons milk, as desired

In a large bowl, beat together the butter or margarine and cream cheese with an electric mixer. With the mixer on low speed, add the powdered sugar, 1 cup at a time, until smooth and creamy. Beat in the vanilla extract.

If you want a thinner frosting for use on cookies, add milk, 1 teaspoon at a time, until desired consistency is achieved.

A good basic frosting for many different cakes.

OATMEAL CAKE

1 cup quick-cooking oats
1¼ cup boiling water
½ cup shortening
1 cup granulated sugar
1 cup brown sugar, packed
2 eggs
1 teaspoon vanilla extract
1½ cup flour
1 teaspoon baking powder
1 teaspoon baking soda
½ teaspoon salt
1 teaspoon ground cinnamon

Crunch topping
6 tablespoons butter or margarine
1 cup brown sugar, packed
¼ cup sweetened condensed milk
½ cup shredded coconut
½ cup walnuts or pecans, chopped

Combine quick-cooking oats and boiling water and let stand 20 minutes. Separately, cream together shortening, granulated sugar, brown sugar, eggs, and vanilla. In another bowl, stir together flour, baking powder, baking soda, salt, and cinnamon, and add to creamed mixture along with soaked oats. Pour into greased and floured 9 x 13-inch baking pan. Bake at 350°F for 35 minutes.

While cake is baking, prepare crunch topping: In a saucepan, mix together all topping ingredients. Cook over low heat until the mixture bubbles. Spread on top of the baked oatmeal cake.

Return cake to oven at about 425°F and bake until topping bubbles, or 5–7 minutes. Remove from oven and let cool.

At our funeral viewings, there is a container with slips of paper for items to bring for the funeral lunch. These slips list things like cake, Jell-O fruit salad, chicken broth (for noodles), and potato salad. These papers are taken by the ladies in our community so we can make the load lighter for the grieving family. This is an example of a cake that we sometimes make for this situation.

I also enjoy making this special cake for potlucks or quilting bees. Our children like plainer cakes like chocolate or white cake, so this one is a treat for me.

SHOOFLY CAKE

2 cups flour
1 cup brown sugar, packed
½ cup butter, softened
1 cup boiling water
½ cup molasses
1 teaspoon baking soda
1/2 teaspoon salt
Confectioner's sugar or whipped cream

Combine flour, brown sugar, and butter by hand to make fine crumbs. Reserve ¾ cup of this crumb mixture to put on top of cake. Separately, mix together boiling water, molasses, and baking soda. Stir into remaining crumb mixture.

Put cake batter in a greased 9 x 13-inch baking pan and sprinkle with reserved crumbs. Bake at 350°F for 30–40 minutes.

Good topped with confectioner's sugar or whipped cream.

This is the cake version of shoofly pie. We think this tastes even better the second day.

VANILLA SPONGE CAKE WITH CHOCOLATE FROSTING

1 cup water

1 cup butter or margarine

2 cups sugar

2⅔ cups flour

Pinch salt

2 eggs

⅔ cup buttermilk

2 teaspoons vanilla extract

1½ teaspoon baking soda

In a saucepan, bring the water to a boil, then add the butter or margarine and remove from heat. In a medium bowl, combine the sugar, flour, and salt. Beat in the hot butter-water mixture. Add the eggs, buttermilk, vanilla, and baking soda and beat well.

Pour into a greased 15 x 10 x 1-inch jelly-roll pan. The batter is thin and will come to the rim of the pan, so be careful when placing in oven. Bake at 350°F for 30–35 minutes, or until toothpick inserted in center comes out clean. Cool completely, then frost with chocolate frosting.

Chocolate frosting

½ cup butter or margarine, melted

⅔ cup cocoa powder

3 cups powdered sugar

⅓ cup milk

1 teaspoon vanilla extract

Stir cocoa powder into melted butter or margarine. Alternately add powdered sugar and milk, beating to spreading consistency.

Add small amount additional milk, if needed. Stir in vanilla.

Makes about 2 cups frosting.

This is a favorite to use for birthday cakes or for the evening meal after hosting church service.

Pies

APPLE CARAMEL CREAM PIE

3 cups apples, peeled, cored, and sliced
1 (9-inch) pie shell, unbaked
½ cup granulated sugar
½ cup brown sugar, packed
1 tablespoon flour
¼ teaspoon salt
3 eggs
½ cup cream
¼ cup dark corn syrup
½ teaspoon vanilla extract
Ground cinnamon

Arrange apples in bottom of pie shell. In a medium bowl, mix together the granulated sugar, brown sugar, flour, salt, eggs, cream, corn syrup, and vanilla. Pour all of the above mixture over the apples. Sprinkle with cinnamon.

Bake at 425°F for 10 minutes. Reduce heat to 350°F and bake until the middle is set, about 50 minutes. Remove, cool, and serve.

Makes 1 (9-inch) pie.

It is nice to try different kinds of apple pies. This might be quite different for some, but it's tasty!

BLUEBERRY CRUMB PIE

¼ cup flour; or 2 teaspoons cornstarch
⅔ cup granulated sugar
2 tablespoons lemon juice
4 cups blueberries
1 (9-inch) pie shell, unbaked

Topping
½ cup flour
⅓ cup brown sugar, packed
⅓ teaspoon ground cinnamon
¼ cup butter, cubed

In a small bowl, stir together the flour or cornstarch and granulated sugar. In another bowl, sprinkle lemon juice over blueberries; stir. Add flour mixture to blueberries, stirring carefully until berries are coated. Spread berries in pie shell. Do not prick crust.

Make topping: Combine flour, brown sugar, cinnamon, and butter. Mix with a pastry cutter or two forks until crumbly. Sprinkle over berries and press down gently.

Bake at 425°F for 20 minutes, then reduce temperature to 350°F and bake for an additional 45 minutes. Cool before cutting and serving.

Makes 1 (9-inch) pie.

CHOCOLATE PECAN PIE

2 ounces unsweetened chocolate

¼ cup butter or margarine

3 eggs

1 cup dark corn syrup

¾ cup sugar

1 teaspoon vanilla extract

⅛ teaspoon salt

1 (9-inch) pie shell, unbaked

1 cup pecan halves

In a small saucepan over low heat, melt chocolate and butter or margarine. In a medium bowl, lightly beat together eggs, corn syrup, and sugar. Add chocolate mixture and stir; then stir in vanilla and salt.

Arrange pecans in bottom of pie shell, then carefully pour chocolate-egg mixture over pecans.

Bake at 350°F for 40–50 minutes, or until knife inserted near center comes out clean. Pie will become firmer as it cooks. Cool completely before serving.

Makes 1 (9-inch) pie.

If you like chocolate and pecans, I'm sure you will like this pie.

CUSTARD PIE

3 eggs, separated
1½ teaspoon vanilla extract
¾ cup sugar
1 tablespoon cornstarch
2 cups milk
1 (9-inch) pie shell, unbaked
Ground nutmeg

Mix egg yolks, vanilla, sugar, and cornstarch together in a small bowl. Heat milk in medium saucepan to boiling, then turn off heat. Remove ½ cup of the hot milk and stir into egg yolk mixture. (This keeps the eggs from cooking when added to the rest of the hot milk.) Pour this mixture into the milk in saucepan and stir until combined.

Beat egg whites until stiff, then stir into milk mixture. Pour into pie shell. Sprinkle nutmeg on top.

Bake at 350°F for 30–35 minutes, or until knife inserted in center of pie comes out clean.

Makes 1 (9-inch) pie.

Our children love Custard Pie. They especially love it when I add fresh fruit to the pie, like raspberries or peaches.

FRENCH RHUBARB PIE

2 cups rhubarb, diced

2 tablespoons flour

1 cup granulated sugar

1 egg, slightly beaten

1 teaspoon vanilla extract

1 (9-inch) pie shell, unbaked

Topping

¾ cup flour

½ cup brown sugar, packed

⅓ cup butter or margarine

In a bowl, stir together rhubarb, 2 tablespoons flour, granulated sugar, egg, and vanilla. Pour mixture into pie shell.

Make topping: In a small bowl, combine ¾ cup flour, brown sugar, and butter or margarine. Cut with pastry cutter or two forks until crumbly. Spread evenly over rhubarb mixture.

Bake at 400°F for 10 minutes, then lower temperature to 350°F and continue cooking 40 minutes, or until topping is lightly browned.

Makes 1 (9-inch) pie.

I have over a dozen rhubarb plants in my garden. It is so good to have a lot of rhubarb on hand for many recipes, and to freeze or can for later.

GRANDMA'S BUTTERSCOTCH PIE

½ cup butter
½ cup brown sugar, packed
1 tablespoon water
3 egg yolks, beaten (reserve whites for meringue topping)
2 cups whole milk
¾ cup granulated sugar
¼ cup flour
1 (9-inch) pie shell, baked

Meringue topping
3 egg whites, at room temperature
¼ teaspoon cream of tartar
6 tablespoons sugar

Melt butter in saucepan, then add brown sugar and water. Cook over medium heat until mixture makes a thick syrup, about 10 minutes. Don't cook it on high or it will burn.

Add a small amount of the cooked syrup to the egg yolks and stir to temper the eggs. Pour this egg mixture into the syrup mixture. Add milk, granulated sugar, and flour. Continue cooking, stirring constantly, until thickened, about 10 minutes. Pour into baked pie shell. The filling will thicken a little more as it cools.

Prepare meringue topping: Beat reserved egg whites and cream of tartar on high until soft peaks begin to form. Add sugar, 1 tablespoon at a time, while still beating. Spread on pie, making sure meringue touches crust all around. Make small peaks in meringue using the back of a spoon.

Bake at 350°F for 10–15 minutes until meringue peaks begin to brown. Cool, then refrigerate until ready to serve.

Makes 1 (9-inch) pie.

I remember the smell of butterscotch pudding while mother cooked it on the kerosene stove. It was one of brother Amos's favorite pies.

PEACH CREAM PIE

2½ cups peaches, peeled, pitted, and sliced
1 cup milk
1 cup sugar
⅓ cup plus 1 tablespoon flour
Pinch salt
1 (9-inch) pie shell, unbaked

In a medium bowl, stir together peaches, milk, sugar, flour, and salt. Pour into pie shell and bake at 400°F for 30 minutes. Reduce oven to 350°F and bake for 30 more minutes.

Cool completely.

Makes 1 (9-inch) pie.

Note: Fresh rhubarb may be substituted for peaches.

We have made peach pies for weddings during the peach harvest season. But we like peaches fixed almost any way.

PECAN PIE

6 eggs, beaten

1½ cup sugar

1 teaspoon salt

1½ cup light corn syrup

1 teaspoon butter, melted

1 teaspoon vanilla extract

1 cup water

2 (9-inch) pie shells, unbaked

2 cups pecans (halves or pieces), divided

Mix together beaten eggs, sugar, salt, corn syrup, butter, vanilla, and water. Divide mixture evenly between the two pie shells. Sprinkle 1 cup pecans on top of each pie.

Bake at 350°F for 10 minutes, then reduce oven to 300°F and bake for an additional 40–50 minutes, or until middle of pie is set.

Cool completely before serving.

Makes 2 (9-inch) pies.

PLAIN APPLE PIE

6 medium apples, peeled, cored and sliced (6 cups)
1 (9-inch) pie shell, unbaked
2 tablespoons flour
1 cup sugar
2 teaspoons ground cinnamon

Place apples in pie shell. In a small bowl, mix together flour, sugar, and cinnamon. Sprinkle flour mixture evenly over apples.

Bake at 400°F for 30 minutes, or until apples are soft.

Makes 1 (9-inch) pie.

This simple pie will always be my favorite apple pie recipe. My mother always made this pie. There is no top crust or topping, just the bottom crust and the filling. It can easily be baked for a quick family dessert.

RHUBARB CUSTARD PIE

3 cups rhubarb, finely chopped
3 eggs, well beaten
1½ cup sugar mixed with 2 tablespoons flour
½ cup half-and-half
1 teaspoon vanilla extract
1 (9-inch) pie shell, unbaked

In a medium bowl, stir together all ingredients except pie shell. Pour mixture into pie shell. Bake at 400°F for 15 minutes, then reduce oven temperature to 350°F and bake for 45 minutes more.

Makes 1 (9-inch) pie.

I only make this pie when we have our own rhubarb to use from the garden. Rhubarb is one of the first signs of spring. It's amazing how quickly it sprouts through the ground.

My husband, Joe, is always happy to see that first rhubarb custard pie on the table each spring. It is very good served warm with ice cream.

SHORTCUT PIE CRUST

1½ cup flour

1 teaspoon sugar

½ teaspoon salt

¼ teaspoon baking powder

½ cup vegetable oil

3 tablespoons cold water (before measuring out, put some water and ice cubes in a small bowl)

Whisk together the flour, sugar, salt, and baking powder. In a separate bowl, whisk together the oil and water, then pour over the dry ingredients. Stir with a fork until the dough is evenly moistened.

Dump dough into pie pan and, using your fingers, press dough across bottom and up sides of pan. The edge is not high on this crust, so pressing a fork along the edges of the crust makes a beautiful, rustic-looking crust. Fill the crust as desired, and bake.

Alternatively, if recipe calls for a prebaked pie shell, after pressing dough into pie pan, poke bottom and sides of crust a few times with a fork and bake at 425°F for 15 minutes. Cool completely, then fill.

Makes 1 (9-inch) pie crust.

This is a quick and easy no-roll pie crust recipe. I love the hint of saltiness in the crust, which compliments sweet pie fillings.

SHOOFLY PIE OR VANILLA PIE

Bottom layer

½ cup brown sugar

¼ cup molasses

¼ cup light corn syrup

1 tablespoon flour

1 egg, beaten

1 cup water

1 teaspoon vanilla extract

1 (9-inch) pie shell, unbaked

Top layer

1 cup flour

½ cup brown sugar

¼ cup butter

½ teaspoon baking soda

½ teaspoon baking powder

Make bottom layer: In a saucepan over medium heat, combine the brown sugar, molasses, corn syrup, flour, egg, water, and vanilla. Cook, stirring constantly, until thickened, about 15 minutes. Pour into pie shell.

Make top layer: Using a pastry cutter or a fork, combine flour, brown sugar, butter, baking soda, and baking powder until crumbly. Sprinkle on top of bottom layer of pie.

Bake at 375°F for 40–45 minutes.

Makes 1 (9-inch) pie.

I personally am not a big fan of shoofly pie, but it is a favorite among many Amish in certain areas. This recipe is sweeter than some and less bold than those using all molasses. Some call it Vanilla Pie.

VANILLA CREAM PIE

¾ cup sugar

3 tablespoons cornstarch

¼ teaspoon salt

2 cups milk

3 egg yolks, slightly beaten (reserve whites for meringue)

2 tablespoons butter

1 teaspoon vanilla extract

1 (9-inch) pie shell, baked

Meringue

3 egg whites, at room temperature

¼ teaspoon cream of tartar

½ teaspoon vanilla extract

6 tablespoons sugar

In a saucepan, combine sugar, cornstarch, and salt. Gradually stir in milk. Cook and stir over medium heat until mixture boils and thickens, then cook 2 minutes longer, stirring constantly. Stir a small amount of hot mixture into beaten egg yolks. Pour this egg mixture into hot milk mixture and cook 2 more minutes, stirring constantly. Remove from heat, stir in butter and vanilla, and pour into baked pie shell.

Make meringue: Beat reserved egg whites with cream of tartar and vanilla on high until soft peaks begin to form. Add sugar, 1 tablespoon at a time, while still beating. Spread on pie, making sure meringue touches the crust all around. Make small peaks in meringue using the back of a spoon.

Bake at 350°F for 12–15 minutes, or until meringue is golden. Cool completely, and refrigerate until ready to serve.

Makes 1 (9-inch) pie.

Cream pies are always loved around here. This pie has a meringue topping, which adds to the delicious taste.

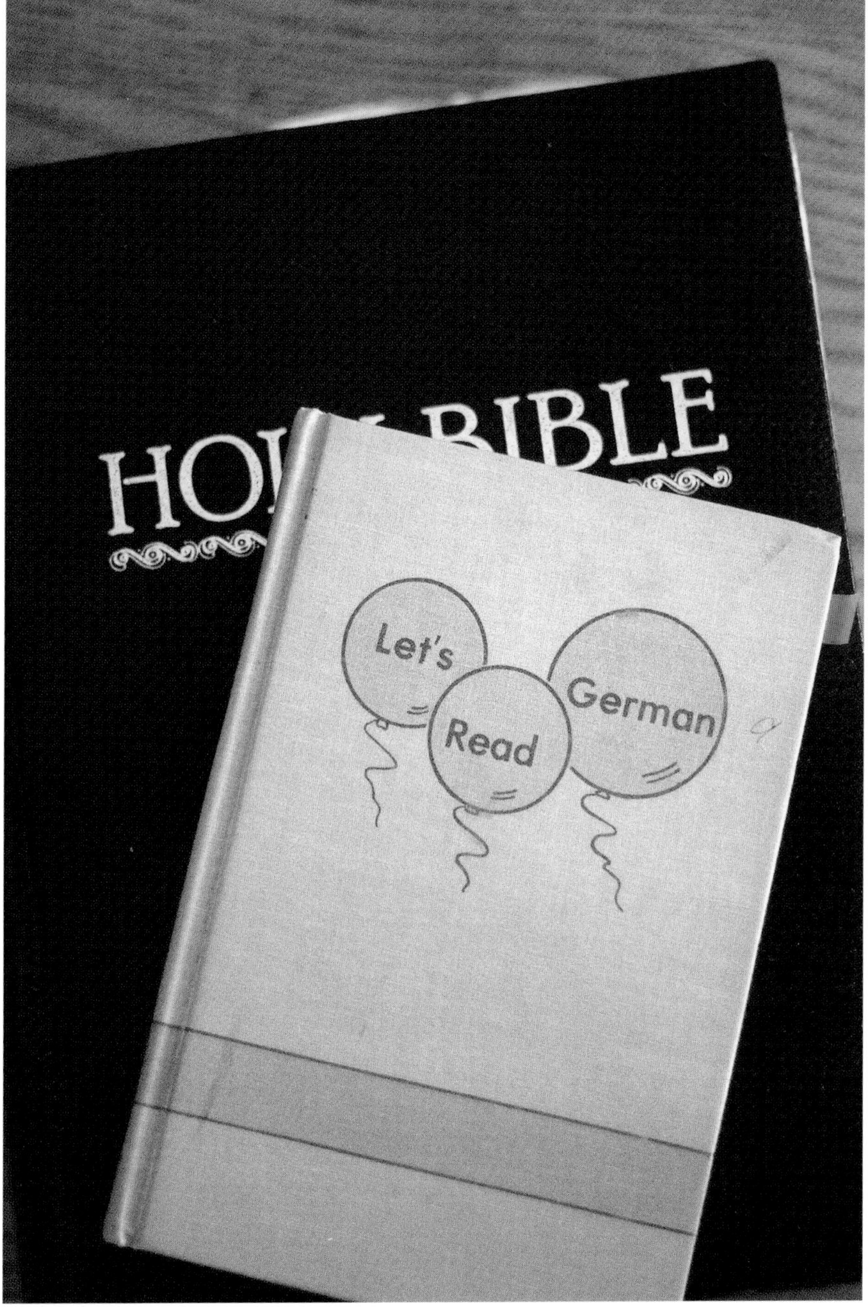
Let's
Read
German

Cookies &
Bars

BANANA COOKIES

1 cup sugar

½ cup butter, softened

½ cup shortening

1 teaspoon vanilla extract

2 eggs

3 ripe bananas, mashed (about 1 cup)

½ cup buttermilk

1½ teaspoon baking soda

½ teaspoon salt

3¼ cups flour

Banana frosting

2 tablespoons butter, melted

1–2 bananas, mashed

3–4 cups powdered sugar

2 tablespoons milk

1 teaspoon vanilla extract

Preheat oven to 350°F. Cream together sugar, butter, shortening, and vanilla until light and fluffy. Mix in eggs and bananas. Mix in buttermilk.

Add baking soda, salt, and flour to mixture, and beat until combined. Do not overbeat; it will be a sticky batter. Drop by teaspoonfuls onto a greased baking sheet. Bake 9–10 minutes, until slightly golden. Cool completely.

Mix all frosting ingredients together and spread on top of cooled cookies. Makes about 4 dozen cookies.

Our youngest son, Kevin, loved bananas as a small child and would get his words mixed up and call out "Monkey, Monkey" when he saw bananas in the grocery store. These cookies remind me of his early confusion!

BANANA WHOOPIE PIES

½ cup (1 stick) unsalted butter, softened

½ cup brown sugar, packed

¼ cup granulated sugar

½ teaspoon salt

1 teaspoon vanilla extract

1½ cup bananas, mashed (3 medium to large)

2 large eggs

2 cups flour

1 teaspoon baking soda

¾ cup chopped walnuts (optional)

Filling

1 (8-ounce) package cream cheese, room temperature

4 tablespoons soft butter

2 cups confectioners' sugar, sifted

1 teaspoon vanilla extract

In a large bowl, cream together the butter, sugars, and salt until light and fluffy. Add vanilla and mashed bananas. The mixture will look curdled; that's okay. Beat in the eggs, one at a time.

Whisk together the flour and baking soda; add to banana mixture. Mix until evenly combined. Scrape bottom and sides of bowl, then mix for 1 minute more. Stir in walnuts.

Scoop the dough by the quarter cup for large cookies, and by the tablespoon for smaller cookies. Allow plenty of space between them.

Bake for 12-14 minutes at 400°F, until the tops spring back when lightly touched with your finger and the edges are a very light golden brown. Remove from the oven and cool on the baking sheet for 10 minutes before transferring the cookies to a rack to finish cooling completely before filling.

Make filling: Beat the cream cheese and butter until smooth and fluffy. Beat in the sugar in two additions. Add the vanilla. Beat for 2 to 3 minutes, until very fluffy.

To make filled whoopie pies, choose two cookies of the same or similar size. Spread a thick layer of filling on the bottom of one cookie, and top with the second cookie.

After we take our turn to host church, it is our tradition to fill a container with treats and give them to the family that is hosting church next. I like to make whoopie pies when it's my turn to fill the container. I wrap them individually in plastic wrap so they don't stick together.

BUTTERMILK COOKIES WITH GLAZED MAPLE NUT FROSTING (AND BACON BITS)

½ cup brown sugar, packed

½ cup granulated sugar

½ cup butter or lard, melted

2 eggs, beaten

½ cup buttermilk

1 teaspoon maple extract

1 teaspoon baking soda

¼ teaspoon cream of tartar

2½ cups flour

¼ cup walnuts, chopped

Glaze

¾ cup powdered sugar

3 tablespoons buttermilk

½ teaspoon maple extract

2–3 slices bacon, fried and finely chopped (optional)

In a bowl, stir together the brown sugar and granulated sugar, then stir in the melted butter and eggs. In another bowl, stir together the buttermilk, maple extract, baking soda, and cream of tartar.

Add half the flour and half the buttermilk mixture to the sugar-egg mixture, stirring well. Stir in the rest of the flour and buttermilk mixture; stir in the walnuts.

Drop teaspoonfuls of dough onto a greased baking sheet. Bake at 375°F for 15–20 minutes. Cool cookies before glazing.

Make glaze: Stir together powdered sugar, buttermilk, and maple extract. When cookies are cooled, spread glaze on top of each cookie. If desired, top with a few bacon bits.

Joe enjoys buttermilk cookies in his lunch box. It's hard to keep these cookies around for long, but they will keep well in a covered container.

CHERRY PIE BARS

1 cup butter, softened

2 cups granulated sugar

4 eggs

1 teaspoon vanilla extract

¼ teaspoon almond extract

3 cups flour

1 teaspoon salt

1 pint homemade cherry pie filling; or 1 (21-ounce) can cherry
pie filling

Glaze

1 cup powdered sugar

½ teaspoon vanilla extract

½ teaspoon almond extract

2 tablespoons milk

Preheat oven to 350°F. Cream together butter and granulated sugar. Add eggs, vanilla, and almond extract, and beat well. Add flour and salt; mix until combined.

Grease a 9 x 13-inch baking pan and spread about three-quarters of the batter in the bottom. Spread pie filling over the batter. Drop remaining batter by teaspoonfuls on top of pie filling. Bake 35–40 minutes, or until toothpick inserted through crust comes out clean.

Combine glaze ingredients and drizzle over the bars. Makes 15 servings.

*If you like cherry pie, you will like these bars.
They are easy to make and hard to keep around.*

CHOCOLATE CHIP BARS

½ cup milk

1 teaspoon white vinegar

1 egg

1 teaspoon vanilla extract

½ cup shortening

1 cup brown sugar

½ teaspoon salt

½ teaspoon baking soda

1¾ cup flour

1 cup chocolate chips

Preheat oven to 350°F. Combine milk and vinegar; let stand 5 minutes. In a large bowl, stir together the milk mixture and remaining ingredients, except for the flour and chocolate chips. Add flour, and mix well. Add chocolate chips. Spread batter evenly over a greased 15 x 10 x 1-inch jelly-roll pan. Bake for 20–25 minutes.

This is something we make often. If we are in a hurry to prepare a quick dessert, it is a simple solution. Anything with chocolate chips in it doesn't last long around our house. This is also a good bar to take to gatherings and reunions. If you have sour milk on hand, you can use it instead of the milk and vinegar as shown in the recipe.

CHURCH SUGAR COOKIES

2½ cups granulated sugar

2½ cups brown sugar, packed

3 cups shortening or lard

4 eggs, beaten

11 cups flour

6 teaspoons baking powder

3 teaspoons baking soda

2 cups milk

1 cup cream

2 teaspoons vanilla extract

2 teaspoons lemon extract

In a very large bowl, cream together granulated sugar, brown sugar, and shortening. Add eggs, mixing well. Separately, sift together flour, baking powder, and baking soda. Alternately add this flour mixture, the milk, and the cream to sugar mixture. Add vanilla and lemon extract, mixing well.

Drop by tablespoonfuls onto baking sheets and bake at 400°F for 10–12 minutes, or until slightly browned.

These taste good with white frosting.

Makes 8 dozen large cookies. Recipe can be halved.

This makes a large batch, so it's a great recipe if you need to bring cookies to a potluck. In our church these would be served at the church lunch, along with a variety of other cookies.

DELICIOUS COOKIES

3½ cups flour

1 teaspoon cream of tartar

1 teaspoon baking soda

1 cup granulated sugar

1 cup brown sugar, packed

1 cup butter or margarine, softened

½ cup vegetable oil

1 egg

2 teaspoons vanilla extract

1 cup chopped pecans or walnuts

1 cup quick-cooking or old-fashioned oats

1 cup crispy rice cereal

1 cup shredded coconut (optional)

Granulated sugar, for coating

Preheat oven to 350°F. In a small bowl, combine flour, cream of tartar, and baking soda. In a large bowl, cream together the granulated sugar, brown sugar, butter or margarine, oil, egg, and vanilla. Gradually beat flour mixture into sugar mixture.

Fold nuts, oats, crispy rice cereal, and coconut, if desired, into cookie dough. Shape into 1-inch balls and place on baking sheet. Dampen the bottom of a flat glass with a wet paper towel, dip into a small bowl of granulated sugar, and press onto cookie round. Repeat for each cookie.

Bake for 10–12 minutes, or until lightly browned.

Makes 6 dozen cookies.

This is a crisp, crunchy cookie that the children like to dip in their milk.

OUTRAGEOUS CHOCOLATE CHIP COOKIES

2 cups granulated sugar

1½ cup brown sugar

2 cups lard, shortening, or butter

4 eggs

2 cups peanut butter

4 cups flour

2 cups quick-cooking or old-fashioned oats

4 teaspoons baking soda

1 teaspoon salt

12 ounces chocolate chips

In a large bowl, cream together the granulated sugar, brown sugar, lard (or shortening or butter), and eggs until well blended. Add the peanut butter, flour, oats, baking soda, and salt. Mix on medium speed until well blended. Fold chocolate chips into mixture. Refrigerate dough for 1 hour.

Roll dough into balls and press lightly onto baking sheet. Bake at 350°F for 10–15 minutes, or until slightly browned. Let stand on baking sheet a few minutes after removing from oven, then cool on wire racks, parchment paper, or paper towels.

Of all the chocolate chip recipes we make, this is the children's favorite!

PEANUT BUTTER DREAM BARS

1 cup brown sugar, lightly packed

1½ cup flour

2 cups quick-cooking oats

½ teaspoon salt

1 teaspoon baking soda

1 cup butter, melted

½ cup peanut butter

1 (14-ounce) can sweetened condensed milk

1 cup chocolate chips

1 cup mini M&M's

Mix together brown sugar, flour, oats, salt, and baking soda. Add melted butter, mixing together. Reserve 1½ cup of this mixture; press the remaining amount into a 9 x 13-inch baking pan. Bake at 375°F for 12 minutes; remove from oven (don't turn off heat).

Mix together peanut butter and sweetened condensed milk. Spread over baked bar layer. Mix chocolate chips and M&M's into reserved mixture, and spread over top of peanut butter layer. Return to oven for 20 minutes. Remove and cool completely before cutting.

When there is a wedding, the cooking preparations begin two days before the wedding. The women who come to help cook are asked to bring some food for lunch or coffee time. We enjoy resting and talking as we eat and fellowship together. Peanut Butter Dream Bars are something I like to make for such times.

PUMPKIN COOKIES

1 cup shortening

2 cups sugar

2 cups pumpkin purée

4 cups all-purpose flour

2 teaspoons baking soda

2 teaspoons baking powder

2 teaspoons ground cinnamon

In a large bowl, cream together the shortening and sugar. Mix in pumpkin purée and cream all together until blended.

Add flour, baking soda, baking powder, and cinnamon. Mix on medium speed until well blended.

Drop by rounded tablespoonfuls onto an ungreased baking sheet. Bake at 350°F for 8–10 minutes, or until centers appear done. Let stand on baking sheet a few minutes before transferring to wire racks to cool.

These are also good frosted.

I make these more in the fall, when there is an abundance of fresh pumpkin. I like to can my extra pumpkin for use throughout the year.

SOFT CHOCOLATE CHIP COOKIES

1 cup butter

¾ cup brown sugar, packed

2 eggs

1 (3.4-ounce) package chocolate or vanilla instant pudding

2¼ cups flour

1 teaspoon baking soda

1 teaspoon vanilla extract

1 (12-ounce) package chocolate chips

1 cup M&M's

In a medium bowl, cream together butter and brown sugar until blended. Add eggs and mix until combined. Add instant pudding, flour, baking soda, and vanilla, and mix well. Stir in chocolate chips.

Place by rounded teaspoonfuls onto ungreased baking sheet. Bake at 350°F for 8 minutes. Remove baking sheet from oven and put a few M&M's on top of each cookie. Return to oven and continue baking another 2–4 minutes, or until edges begin to brown.

Remove from oven and leave on baking sheet a few minutes. Use a spatula to place on wire racks to finish cooling.

These cookies are cake-like in texture. The flavor will change a little depending on whether you use chocolate or vanilla pudding.

SWISS ROLL BARS

2 eggs
½ cup vegetable oil
2 cups applesauce
2 cups flour
1½ cup sugar
½ cup unsweetened cocoa powder
¼ teaspoon salt
1 teaspoon baking soda

Filling
1 (16-ounce) container whipped topping
1 (8-ounce) package cream cheese
1½ cup powdered sugar

Topping
5 tablespoons butter
1 (12-ounce) package chocolate chips

In large bowl, beat the eggs, oil, applesauce, flour, sugar, cocoa powder, salt, and baking soda on medium speed until well blended. Line two 15 x 10 x 1-inch jelly-roll pans with parchment paper. Divide the batter evenly between the two pans, spreading to the edges of the pans. Bake at 350°F for 25–30 minutes. Cool completely before assembling layers.

Prepare filling: In a medium bowl, mix the whipped topping, cream cheese, and powdered sugar on medium speed until well blended. Spread on top of one of the cooled cakes. Remove the other cake from the pan and place on top of filling.

In a small saucepan, melt butter and chocolate chips on low, stirring constantly, until chips are melted. Spread on top of filled cake. Refrigerate and cut into bars.

Sometimes our children ask for this instead of a cake for their birthday. We put candles and write "Happy Birthday" on top just like a regular cake! This cake (or bars) need to be kept refrigerated because of the filling.

Desserts &
Candies

APPLE CRISP

9 cups apples, peeled and sliced
1 cup sugar
2 tablespoons ground cinnamon

Crumb topping
¾ cup butter or margarine, cubed
1½ cup sugar
2 cups flour
2 tablespoons ground cinnamon

In a large bowl, toss together apples, sugar, and cinnamon. Pour into buttered 9 x 13-inch baking dish.

In a large bowl, combine all crumb topping ingredients with a pastry cutter or two forks, mixing until coarse. Spread over apples.

Bake at 350°F for 45–50 minutes, or until browned and bubbly and apples are tender.

This is one of my mom's original recipes. We would pour cold milk on the warm crisp. Now we serve ice cream with it, but when I was young, we didn't have a refrigerator so we couldn't keep ice cream.

APPLE DANISH DESSERT

3 cups flour

½ teaspoon salt

1 cup shortening

½ cup milk

1 egg, separated

6 cups apples, peeled, cored, and
sliced (Golden Delicious, Braeburn,
or Granny Smith work well)

1 cup sugar

1 teaspoon ground cinnamon

4 tablespoons butter

Glaze

1½ cup powdered sugar

⅛ teaspoon salt

1 teaspoon vanilla extract

2–3 tablespoons milk

In a medium bowl, combine flour and salt. Cut shortening into flour mixture with a pastry cutter or two forks until the mixture resembles coarse cornmeal. In a small bowl, lightly beat together milk and egg yolk (reserve egg white, for brushing dough). Add to flour mixture and stir until well combined.

Take half the dough and roll out on slightly floured surface to fit a 15 x 11 x 1-inch jelly-roll pan. Put dough in baking pan and pat into place so that entire pan is covered in crust.

Arrange sliced apples on crust. In a small bowl, mix together sugar and cinnamon, then sprinkle over apples. Dot with butter.

Roll out remaining dough and use it to cover apples. Beat reserved egg white lightly and brush over top of dough. Bake at 375°F for 45 minutes.

In a small bowl, combine all glaze ingredients. While Danish is still warm, spread glaze over top. Can be served with ice cream.

Recipes with apples always remind me of when I was young. We would get together with my uncle Chris and family and peel apples to prepare for making apple butter the next day. Uncle Chris had a large copper kettle, and the butter would be cooked outside over an open fire. The butter would then be canned.

DATE-NUT PUDDING (TRIFLE)

1 (8-ounce) package dates
1 teaspoon baking soda
1 cup boiling water
¼ cup shortening
1 cup sugar
1 egg
1 teaspoon vanilla extract
1⅔ cup flour
½ teaspoon salt
½ cup nuts
½ cup raisins
Whipped cream, for layering

Pit and quarter dates, and place in a bowl. Add baking soda and pour boiling water over dates. Let stand until completely cooled.

In a separate bowl, cream together shortening, sugar, and egg until well blended. Add cooled date mixture, vanilla, flour, salt, nuts, and raisins. Stir until well blended.

Spread batter into greased and floured 9 x 13-inch pan and bake for 30–35 minutes at 350°F.

Remove from oven and cool completely. Cut into 1-inch squares. Put a layer of squares into a glass dessert bowl. Add a layer of whipped cream, then another layer of squares. Continue layers until all the squares are used up, ending with a layer of whipped cream. A few additional nuts can be sprinkled on top.

Can also just be cut into serving-sized pieces and topped with whipped cream.

This is similar to another recipe called Cinnamon Pudding. I think my mom would substitute cinnamon for dates when she didn't have any dates in the house. This special dessert is sometimes served at weddings.

HOMEMADE CHEESECAKE

3 cups graham cracker crumbs

½ cup butter, melted

1 cup sugar, divided

1 (3-ounce) package Jell-O™

1 cup boiling water

8 ounces cream cheese

1 teaspoon vanilla extract

1 (12-ounce) can evaporated milk; or 1⅔ cup heavy cream

In a bowl, mix graham cracker crumbs, melted butter, and ½ cup sugar. Separately, dissolve Jell-O™ in boiling water. Refrigerate until slightly thickened.

Cream together cream cheese, remaining ½ cup sugar, and vanilla. Add refrigerated Jell-O™ and beat well. Whip evaporated milk or heavy cream until stiff; fold into cream cheese mixture. Pack two-thirds of graham mixture on the bottom of a 9 x 13-inch pan. Add cream cheese filling and sprinkle with remaining graham mixture. Refrigerate and serve.

This is sometimes served at Amish weddings, although cheesecake is a good dessert with any meal. It can be made ahead of time. I like to use orange or cherry gelatin once in a while to flavor it, but my favorite is lemon. Or you can serve it with fresh fruit—put strawberries or blueberries on top.

HOMEMADE ICE CREAM

7 eggs
3½ cups sugar
1 (5.1-ounce) package vanilla instant pudding
1 teaspoon salt
10 cups milk
4 teaspoons vanilla extract

Beat eggs, then add remaining ingredients. Mix together. Freeze in your ice cream maker according to the manufacturer's directions.

When we make ice cream, we use a hand-cranked ice cream freezer. We use ice and salt to harden it in the ice cream freezer, and in the winter we even use snow!

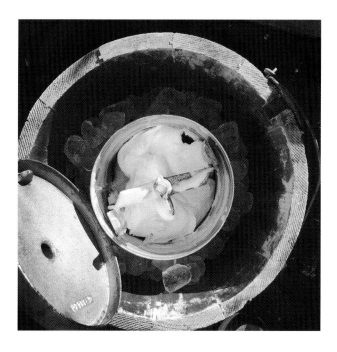

LEMON PUDDING DESSERT

1 cup butter or margarine, melted

1½ cup flour

½ cup sugar

½ cup pecans, finely chopped

1 cup powdered sugar

8 ounces cream cheese

1 (8-ounce) container whipped topping, divided

2 (3.4 ounce) packages lemon instant pudding

3 cups milk

Stir together melted butter or margarine, flour, sugar, and pecans. Mixture should be crumbly. Press into buttered 9 x 13-inch pan. Bake at 375°F for 15 minutes, or until golden brown. Let cool.

Cream together powdered sugar and cream cheese. Stir in 1 cup whipped topping. Put large tablespoonfuls of cream cheese mixture on cooled crust, then carefully spread mixture across entire crust.

Beat together instant pudding and milk; pour on top of cream cheese layer. Refrigerate for about 1 hour until set, then top with remaining whipped topping.

Keep refrigerated until ready to serve.

You can use any pudding flavor for this dessert. Our children really like it when I make it with chocolate pudding.

PEACH COBBLER

½ cup butter

2 cups sugar

2 cups flour

1 tablespoon baking powder

1½ cup milk

4 cups peaches, sliced (fresh or canned)

Preheat oven to 325°F. Put butter in 9 x 13-inch baking pan and place in oven to melt for 3–4 minutes.

Combine sugar, flour, baking powder, and milk. Pour into pan with melted butter. Arrange peaches on top of batter. Bake at 325°F for 35–40 minutes until golden brown.

Can be served with ice cream or milk.

When I need to remove the skin from peaches to use for baking, I place them in a bowl and pour boiling water over top of the peaches. After a minute or two in the hot water, the skin will just slip off.

PEANUT BRITTLE

2 cups sugar

½ teaspoon salt

1 cup light corn syrup

½ cup cold water

2 cups raw peanuts

2 tablespoons butter, softened

1 teaspoon baking soda

Grease a large baking sheet; set aside.

In a heavy 2-quart saucepan over medium heat, bring to a boil sugar, salt, corn syrup, and water. Stir until sugar is dissolved. Stir in peanuts. Set candy thermometer in place and continue cooking. Stir frequently until temperature reaches 300°F, or until a small amount of mixture dropped into very cold water separates into hard and brittle threads.

Remove from heat; immediately stir in butter and baking soda; pour at once onto baking sheet. With two forks, lift and pull peanut mixture into rectangle about 12 x 14 inches in size. Allow to cool, then break candy into pieces.

My dad loved peanut brittle. My mom would always make it around the Christmas holiday.

PEANUT BUTTER CRACKER FUDGE

2 cups sugar
2 tablespoons butter
½ cup milk
1 cup peanut butter
1 teaspoon vanilla extract
1 sleeve saltine crackers, crushed (about 40 crackers)

In a saucepan, bring sugar, butter, and milk to a boil and boil for
1 minute, stirring frequently. Remove from heat and add peanut butter,
vanilla, and crushed saltines.

Spread into a greased 8 x 8-inch baking pan and allow to cool. Cut into
squares.

*Until I made this recipe, I wouldn't have thought that crackers would
taste good in fudge. But the peanut butter, cracker, and sugar combination makes for a nice sweet-and-salty treat.*

STRAWBERRY SHORTCAKE CUPCAKES

1 quart fresh strawberries, cleaned, hulled, and thinly sliced
2 tablespoons sugar
1½ cup flour
⅔ cup additional sugar
2 teaspoons baking powder
½ teaspoon salt
¼ cup butter   **Topping:**
1 egg   1 cup heavy whipping cream
½ cup milk   2 tablespoons sugar
1 teaspoon vanilla extract   1 teaspoon vanilla extract

In a small bowl, combine the strawberries and 2 tablespoons sugar. Stir well; mash half the berries with a potato masher to create some juice. Let set in refrigerator while mixing and baking the shortcake.

In a separate bowl, combine the flour, ⅔ cup additional sugar, baking powder, and salt. Cut the butter into this mixture with pastry cutter or fork until mixture is crumbly.

In a small bowl, beat together egg, milk, and vanilla with a whisk or fork. Stir into flour mixture just until moistened.

Fill 8 greased muffin cups two-thirds full. (Paper cupcake liners may be used instead of greasing the muffin tin.) Bake at 425°F for 12 minutes, or until golden brown. Remove from pan and place on wire rack to cool.

Beat whipping cream and sugar on high until soft peaks form. Add vanilla and beat one more minute.

Just before serving, split the shortcakes in half horizontally. Spoon berries and whipped topping between layers and on top.

This is a great dessert, especially when strawberries are in season. It also tastes good served with ice cream. A purchased whipped topping can be used instead of home-whipped cream. The shortcakes are more like biscuits than cakes. Some people enjoy with milk poured over.

Snacks & Beverages

CHEESE BALL

2 (8-ounce) packages cream cheese, softened
2 (2-ounce) packages dried ham or beef, chopped
1 small onion, finely chopped
Salt, to taste

Mix together all ingredients. Form into a ball. Refrigerate for a few hours for better flavor. Very good with crackers.

Note: Dried ham or beef is generally available in the refrigerated deli section.

This is our favorite cheese ball. We always made it when I was growing up. We like it with a variety of crackers.

FRESH CORN SALSA

1 cup fresh corn kernels, cooked
4 medium tomatoes, seeded and chopped
¼ cup red onion, finely chopped
¼ cup fresh cilantro, chopped
1 jalapeño pepper, seeded and finely chopped
1 (15-ounce) can black beans, drained and rinsed
¼ cup prepared Italian salad dressing

Combine all ingredients in a bowl and mix well. Serve with tortilla chips.

A different way to make salsa. The corn and red onions make it colorful.

CRISPY SQUARES

1 cup sugar
1 cup light corn syrup
1 cup creamy peanut butter
6 cups crispy rice cereal
1 cup semisweet chocolate chips
1 cup butterscotch chips

In a saucepan, bring sugar and corn syrup to a boil, stirring frequently. Remove from heat, add peanut butter, and stir until peanut butter is melted. Put crispy rice cereal in a large bowl, pour hot mixture over cereal, and stir until well combined.

Butter a 9 x 13-inch baking pan. Pour cereal mixture into pan and press down, spreading evenly.

In a small saucepan, melt chocolate chips and butterscotch chips over low heat. Pour melted chips over cereal and spread evenly. Cool a few hours to firm chocolate, or place in refrigerator to set faster. Cut into small bars.

I make rice crispy treats often, but sometimes I make this recipe for a change. My children really enjoy them.

THICK AND CHUNKY SALSA

14 pounds tomatoes, scalded, peeled, and chopped

10 green bell peppers, chopped

5 cups onions, chopped

2–3 jalapeño peppers, seeded and chopped

1 cup white vinegar

½ cup brown sugar, packed

¼ cup salt

2 teaspoons dried oregano

3 teaspoons chili powder

10 tablespoons Clear Jel

3 cups water

In a large pot, mix together the tomatoes, bell peppers, onions, jalapeño peppers, vinegar, brown sugar, salt, oregano, and chili powder. Cook on low heat for 45 minutes, stirring occasionally. In a separate bowl, mix the Clear Jel and water until dissolved. Add the Clear Jel mixture to the pot and cook for 5 more minutes.

To can the salsa, ladle into hot pint jars, leaving ½-inch headspace. Wipe jar rims with a dampened paper towel. Adjust lids and process in a boiling-water canner for 20 minutes.

The salsa may also be frozen for later use. If you are making a smaller batch to eat rather than can or freeze, cool to room temperature and serve.

Makes 10–12 pint jars.

Note: Clear Jel is a type of food starch you can purchase to use as a thickening agent in canning recipes. It thickens food evenly (without lumps) even when cooked at high temperatures in the canning process. You can find Clear Jel at bulk food stores and online.

Canning times are subject to change according to USDA regulations. For the latest canning times, check your county extension office or the National Center for Home Food Preservation website.

I have made gallons and gallons of this salsa. I always can it. We use this on tacos, haystacks, scrambled eggs, and breakfast burritos, in addition to the usual chips and salsa. A tasty salsa!

M&M'S GRANOLA BARS

2 cups quick-cooking oats
1 cup crispy rice cereal
½ cup brown sugar, packed
½ cup honey
¾ cup peanut butter
¾ cup M&M's

In a bowl, mix all ingredients together with a wooden spoon or spatula. Press into well-greased 9 x 13-inch baking pan.

Bake at 350°F for 18 minutes. Cool briefly, and cut into small squares or rectangles while still warm.

These are a great choice over store-bought snacks. They are quick to make and require only one bowl, so the recipe is easy on cleanup.

MOZZARELLA STICKS

2 eggs

1 tablespoon water

1 cup dry bread crumbs

2½ teaspoons Italian seasoning

½ teaspoon garlic powder

⅛ teaspoon ground pepper

12 sticks string cheese

3 tablespoons flour

3 tablespoons butter, melted

1 cup marinara or spaghetti sauce

In a small bowl, beat together eggs and water. In a resealable plastic bag, combine bread crumbs, Italian seasoning, garlic powder, and pepper. Coat cheese sticks in flour, then dip in egg mixture, and then bread crumb mixture. Dip in both egg and bread crumb mixture a second time to coat thoroughly.

Cover and refrigerate for at least 4 hours, or overnight. Place on ungreased baking sheet. Drizzle with butter. Bake, uncovered, at 400°F for 6–8 minutes, or until heated through. Allow to stand for 3–5 minutes before serving. Use marinara or spaghetti sauce for dipping.

Tip: Regular block mozzarella cheese can be used instead of buying the string cheese sticks; cut block cheese into 4 x ½-inch sticks. These can be frozen before the baking process so they work better.

Mozzarella sticks are something we enjoy for a treat with pizza, or if the children have friends overnight, or to celebrate a birthday. I don't usually make them just for us. We like dipping them in pizza sauce.

POPCORN BALLS

¼ cup butter
1 cup brown sugar, packed
¼ cup light corn syrup
1 teaspoon baking soda
16 cups popped popcorn, salted

Combine butter, brown sugar, and corn syrup in a medium saucepan. Bring to a rolling boil and boil for 2 minutes. Add the baking soda and stir well.

Place popcorn in a large bowl and pour cooked mixture over popcorn, mixing well. Form into 3-inch balls and set on waxed paper to cool.

For color, a few drops of food color can be added to cooked mixture before pouring over popcorn.

My mother would always make Popcorn Balls around Christmastime. I like to add the red and green food color when I make them during the holiday season to give them that Christmas look.

NO-BAKE PEANUT BUTTER CORNFLAKE BARS

½ cup sugar
½ cup light corn syrup
1 cup crunchy peanut butter
3 cups cornflakes cereal, crushed
2 cups chocolate chips

Heat sugar and corn syrup in a large saucepan over medium heat until sugar is melted, then add peanut butter and stir until smooth. Remove pan from heat and stir in crushed cornflakes cereal.

Gently pat mixture into a lightly greased 8 x 8-inch pan. (I line my pan with aluminum foil and then lightly spray it. When it is time to cut the bars, the foil lifts right out.)

Melt chocolate chips over low heat or in the microwave and spread over top. Cool until firm.

A very easy bar to make for a quick snack.

QUICK CARAMEL CORN

1 cup butter

2 cups dark brown sugar, packed

½ cup light corn syrup

½ cup molasses

1 teaspoon vanilla extract

½ teaspoon salt

2 teaspoons baking soda

6 quarts popped popcorn

Melt butter in a 4-quart saucepan. Add brown sugar and corn syrup. Heat to boiling and boil for 3 minutes, stirring frequently. Add the molasses and boil for an additional 2 minutes, continuing to stir frequently.

Remove from heat and add vanilla, salt, and baking soda, stirring briskly. Pour over popped corn and stir until popcorn is thoroughly coated.

Our family likes popcorn fixed almost any way. This is a favorite!

RHUBARB JUICE

8 pounds rhubarb, washed and diced

8 quarts water

2 (12-ounce) cans frozen orange juice

2 (46-ounce) cans pineapple juice

4 cups sugar

2 (3-ounce) packages strawberry gelatin

Combine rhubarb and water and cook until rhubarb is soft, about 25–30 minutes. Strain liquid into a bowl, discarding rhubarb. Add the orange juice, pineapple juice, sugar, and gelatin to the rhubarb juice. Stir until the sugar is dissolved.

Serve the juice as is, or add club soda or ginger ale, or mix with additional pineapple juice.

The juice may be frozen or canned. To can, heat the juice to 190°F. Ladle into hot quart jars, leaving ¼-inch headspace. Wipe jar rims with a dampened paper towel and adjust lids. Process quart jars in a boiling-water canner for 20 minutes.

Makes 8–10 quart jars.

Note: Canning times are subject to change according to USDA regulations. For the latest canning times, check your county extension office or the National Center for Home Food Preservation website.

This is a good thirst-quencher on hot, humid summer days. Sometimes I add one more box of gelatin and one can less of pineapple juice.

TEA CONCENTRATE

6 cups water, divided
1 cup tea leaves of your choice, packed
1½ cup sugar

Boil 4 cups water. Add tea leaves. Put the lid on the pot and remove from heat. Let stand 10–15 minutes. Put sugar in a 2-quart bowl. Strain liquid into bowl, stirring until sugar is dissolved. Rinse leaves with 2 cups cold water, then strain and add this liquid to the sugar liquid. Cool, then measure out 1 cup concentrate into individual containers, and freeze.

To serve, add 1 cup concentrate to 2 quarts cold water.

We grow our own mint for tea. We have spearmint and peppermint that come up every year, so we enjoy fresh tea in the summer months. This concentrate is good to have on hand once the mint plants freeze out in the fall.

VEGETABLE DIP

1 cup sour cream
½ cup mayonnaise
1½ teaspoon dried dill weed
1½ teaspoon seasoned salt

In a medium bowl, mix all the ingredients together. Cover and refrigerate at least 1 hour before serving. You can also make it the day before to allow the flavors to fully meld together.

Serve with cut-up fresh vegetables such as carrots, celery, cucumber, broccoli, cauliflower, mushrooms, or snap peas.

The children eat more healthy, fresh vegetables when I serve vegetables with this dip.

Relishes, Pickles, Jams, & Jellies

BREAD AND BUTTER PICKLES

6 quarts fresh pickling cucumbers, unpeeled and sliced

2 large onions, sliced

½ cup salt

Syrup

5 cups white vinegar

2 cups water

5 cups sugar

1 tablespoon celery seed

1 tablespoon mustard seed

1 teaspoon ground turmeric

Combine cucumbers, onions, and salt, cover with cold water, and let stand 3 hours. Boil syrup ingredients together until clear. Drain cucumbers and onions and combine with the syrup.

Ladle into hot pint jars, leaving ¼-inch headspace. Wipe jar rims with a dampened paper towel. Adjust lids and process in a boiling-water canner for 10 minutes.

Makes about 10 pint jars.

Note: Canning times are subject to change according to USDA regulations. For the latest canning times, check your county extension office or the National Center for Home Food Preservation website.

KETCHUP (FOR CANNING)

8 quarts thick tomato juice

2½ cups white vinegar

1 tablespoon minced pickling spice

2 large onions, chopped

8 cups sugar

12 tablespoons Perma-Flo

7 tablespoons salt

½ teaspoon ground cinnamon

½ teaspoon ground cloves

Boil together the tomato juice, vinegar, pickling spice, and onions until onions are soft. Press through a sieve and put liquid back on the stove to boil for about 1 hour.

Mix together the sugar, Perma-Flo, salt, cinnamon, and cloves. Stir into the tomato mixture and boil an additional 10–15 minutes. Ladle into hot pint jars, leaving ¼-inch headspace. Wipe jar rims with a dampened paper towel. Adjust lids and process in a boiling-water canner for 10 minutes.

Makes 10–12 pint jars.

Note: Perma-Flo is a clear thickener made from corn starch. It is like Clear Jel, but has a slightly creamier consistency. Cooks use Perma-Flo because it prevents food from becoming watery when frozen and then thawed. It is available from bulk food stores and online.

Canning times are subject to change according to USDA regulations. For the latest canning times, check your county extension office or the National Center for Home Food Preservation website.

If I have plenty of tomatoes from the garden, I like to can my own ketchup, pizza sauce, and spaghetti sauce.

FREEZER PICKLES

2 quarts fresh pickling cucumbers, unpeeled and sliced

1 large onion, sliced

2 tablespoons salt

1¾ cup sugar

½ cup white vinegar

Put sliced cucumbers, onion, and salt in a large bowl and refrigerate for 24 hours. Drain after the 24 hours. Whisk together sugar and vinegar and pour over cucumbers. Cover and refrigerate 24 more hours.

Pack pickles in freezer-safe containers. Pour pickle syrup over, leaving a little headspace in each container. Freeze. Will keep in freezer up to 6 months.

I like to be able to freeze some of my pickle recipes because I can reuse the containers and don't have to buy new lids as I do when I can in jars. I always serve these at our lunch when we host church services. I get a lot of compliments because they stay so crisp.

GARDEN SANDWICH SPREAD

6 green tomatoes

6 green bell peppers, seeded and chopped

6 red bell peppers, seeded and chopped

1 medium onion, finely chopped

½ cup prepared yellow mustard

¼ cup sugar

2 tablespoons salt

1½ teaspoon celery seed

2 cups whipped salad dressing

Put the tomatoes and bell peppers through a hand-grinder, or pulse in a food processor to a medium grind.

Place ground-up tomatoes and peppers in a large pot, along with the onion, mustard, sugar, salt, and celery seed. Stir until smooth and yellow in color. Bring to a boil over medium heat and boil for 15 minutes, stirring frequently.

Remove the pot from stove and add the whipped salad dressing, mixing well. The mixture will turn a lighter yellow color. Keep refrigerated.

Makes about 4 cups. Double recipe if preparing for a large group or event.

This is very good on sandwiches. It is also quite colorful with the red and green peppers.

GREEN TOMATO JAM

6 cups green tomatoes, ground in hand-grinder or food processor
4 cups sugar
2 (3-ounce) packages raspberry or strawberry gelatin

In a large saucepan, mix green tomatoes and sugar. Bring to a boil over medium heat and boil for 20 minutes, stirring frequently. Remove from heat and stir in gelatin.

Ladle into hot pint jars, leaving ¼-inch headspace. Wipe jar rims with a dampened paper towel. Adjust lids and process in a boiling-water canner for 10 minutes.

Makes 6–7 pint jars.

Note: Canning times are subject to change according to USDA regulations. For the latest canning times, check your county extension office or the National Center for Home Food Preservation website.

Here is a good way to use up green tomatoes in the garden at the end of the season. The strawberry gelatin makes it taste close to strawberry jam.

HOT PEPPER BUTTER

42 jalapeño peppers, destemmed
2 cups prepared yellow mustard
4 cups white vinegar
6 cups sugar
1 tablespoon salt
1 cup flour
1½ cup water

Grind the peppers. Place ground peppers in a large pot and add the mustard, vinegar, sugar, and salt. Bring to a boil, stirring frequently. Separately, combine the flour and water to make a paste; add to the pepper mixture. Cook for 5 minutes.

Ladle the pepper butter into hot pint jars, leaving ¼-inch headspace. Wipe jar rims with a dampened paper towel. Adjust lids and process in a boiling-water canner for 10 minutes.

Makes 7 pints.

Note: Use plastic gloves when handling the peppers and seeds to avoid burning your skin (particularly if you will be handling babies after cooking).

Canning times are subject to change according to USDA regulations. For the latest canning times, check your county extension office or the National Center for Home Food Preservation website.

This recipe takes a lot of hot chile peppers. I like to use jalapeño or serrano peppers for this butter. It is hot and spicy and is good spread on sandwiches. My mother, Elizabeth, never grew hot peppers or canned them until we met Joe's family. Joe's dad would serve hot peppers with the church lunch, and that's where my parents learned to like them. They started growing and canning their own peppers, as in this butter.

PEACH BUTTER

4 pounds ripe peaches
1 cup water
2 cups granulated sugar
Juice of 1 lemon

Cut a small X in the bottom of each peach. Dip each peach into a pot of boiling water for 30 seconds, and then into a bowl of cold water for 1 minute. The peels should slide right off.

Halve peaches and remove the pits, then cut each half into quarters. Place peach chunks and water in a large pot and bring to a boil. Simmer until peaches are tender, 15–20 minutes, stirring occasionally to ensure they cook evenly. Put cooked peaches in a food processor, or blend with an immersion blender. You can also run them through a food mill (in which case you don't need to peel them before cooking).

Return the peaches to the large pot, add the sugar and lemon juice, and bring the mixture to a strong simmer/gentle boil, cooking for 30–40 minutes, stirring occasionally in the beginning and more often near the end. The butter is usually done when a wooden spoon leaves a clear trail when scraped across the bottom.

If not canning the butter, let it cool, then refrigerate in an airtight container. It should be good for at least 2 weeks.

To can, pour hot butter into hot sterilized quart jars, leaving ½-inch headspace. Wipe jar rims with a dampened paper towel. Adjust lids and process in a boiling-water canner for 10 minutes.

Note: Canning times are subject to change according to USDA regulations. For the latest canning times, check your county extension office or the National Center for Home Food Preservation website.

A different but good way to use your peaches. Similar to apple butter, but with the wonderful flavor of peaches.

PIZZA SAUCE (TO CAN)

4 quarts tomato juice

1½ cup white distilled vinegar

2 cups sugar

1 teaspoon dry mustard

2 tablespoons salt

3 tablespoons onion powder

1 teaspoon ground cinnamon

½ teaspoon hot red pepper flakes

2 teaspoons Italian seasoning

½ teaspoon garlic powder

6 tablespoons Clear Jel

In a large pot, stir together all ingredients except Clear Jel. Bring to a boil, then turn down to a simmer and cook for 1 hour, stirring occasionally.

After 1 hour, stir in the Clear Jel, and cook for an additional 10 minutes. Ladle the sauce into hot pint jars, leaving ½-inch headspace. Wipe jar rims with a dampened paper towel. Adjust lids and process in a boiling-water canner for 10 minutes.

Keeps in the refrigerator for up to two weeks if not canned.

Makes about 8 pints.

Note: Canning times are subject to change according to USDA regulations. For the latest canning times, check your county extension office or the National Center for Home Food Preservation website.

We use a lot of pizza sauce in a year's time, so I like to can quite a few pints. We use it in our pizza casserole and on homemade pizza.

PICKLE RELISH

4 quarts cucumbers

2 cups yellow onions (about 3 onions)

½ cup salt

1 cup water

3 cups vinegar

6 cups sugar

3 teaspoons celery seed

3 teaspoons dry mustard

3 teaspoons ground turmeric

Grind cucumbers and onions in a hand-grinder or food processor. In a large bowl, combine cucumbers, onions, and salt. Let stand for 3 hours, then drain well.

In a large pot, boil water, vinegar, and sugar. Add celery seed, mustard, and turmeric. Add drained cucumber mixture. Cook on medium heat for about 10 minutes.

Ladle the relish into hot pint jars, leaving ¼-inch headspace. Wipe jar rims with a dampened paper towel. Adjust lids and process in a boiling-water canner for 10 minutes.

Makes 7 pint jars. A smaller batch can be made and will keep well in the refrigerator.

Note: Canning times are subject to change according to USDA regulations. For the latest canning times, check your county extension office or the National Center for Home Food Preservation website.

This is good to use on hot dogs and sandwiches. When I add Miracle Whip to it, it also makes a good tartar sauce.

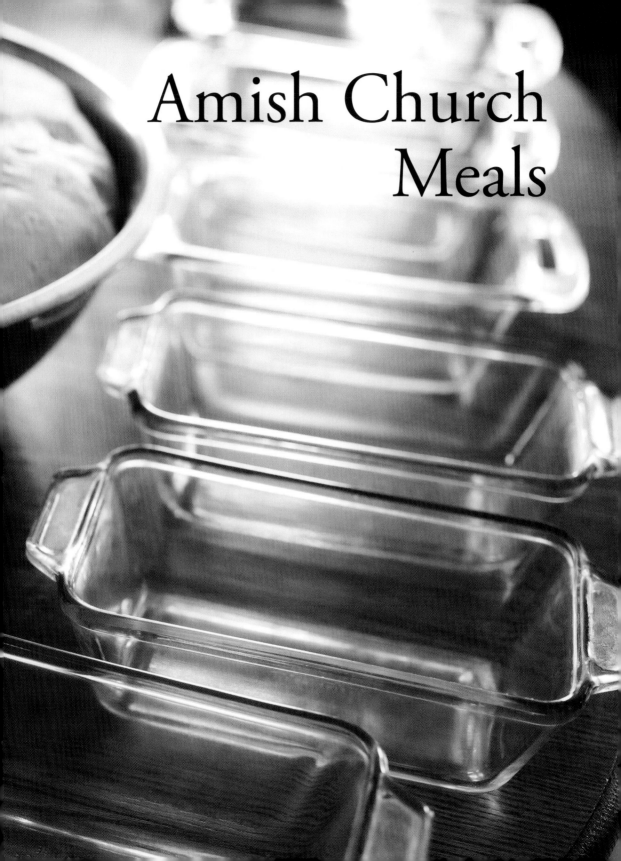

Amish Church Meals

AMISH CHURCH SERVICES

*I*n most Amish communities, our congregations do not meet in a church building, but meet instead in homes, barns, and storage or "pole" buildings as shown here. Church is held every other week, and hosting rotates to various families. Preparing for church includes deep cleaning our homes inside and out, upstairs and down. We generally wash all the windows and curtains, plus all the walls and ceilings. We also clean the furniture. All the children and many relatives are expected to help prepare as they are able. If the services are held in the barn or a storage building or shop, it also means getting that space clean and organized.

Others pitch in to help with food for whomever is preparing to host. One day while cleaning our place for church, our supper was sent over by neighbors Marlin and Janie. This was so thoughtful and very much appreciated.

The evening before, our neighbors Joas and Susan brought supper in. What a treat to not have to make supper!

On Saturday, friends and family also help set up for the services. Helpers make room in the barn to tie all the horses. If the family hosting church doesn't have a big enough barn, others will bring horse blankets for their horses on cold days while they stand outside.

Church also means large amounts of food to prepare. The food is usually sandwiches and not complicated or fancy—things that can be prepared before Sunday itself. The menu for church usually includes homemade white and wheat bread, peanut butter spread (with marshmallow cream in it), homemade church cheese spread, egg salad, pickled red beets, pickles, and cookies. Sometimes we include summer sausage, ham, bologna, and cheeses. We also have jam, butter, tea, and coffee. Younger children often get hot noodle soup. Hosts make popcorn after lunch for everyone after the dishes are almost done.

Afterward, all the women pitch in to help get the dishes washed and back into the totes. The dishes sometimes are supplied, along with the church bench wagon. Our church has a new bench wagon, which also has four 6-foot tables we set up to wash dishes or prepare food. The men help move the benches and Amish hymnals, the *Ausbund*, into the bench wagon.

Holding services in homes is a lot of work but keeps our community spirit going.

All the recipes and quantities listed in this "Amish Church Meals" chapter are for food served after typical Amish church services, but vary from one community to the next. The quantities in these recipes would be multiplied to serve the expected number of people. (To try these for smaller groups, halve or quarter the recipes.)

EGG SALAD

3 pounds hot dogs (may substitute ham)
2½ dozen hard-cooked eggs, peeled and chopped
2 cups whipped salad dressing
2 cups mayonnaise
¼ cup onions, finely chopped
⅓ cup celery, finely chopped
Salt and pepper, to taste

Grind the hot dogs in a grinder. Place ground hot dogs in a large bowl, and stir in the hard-cooked eggs, whipped salad dressing, mayonnaise, onions, and celery until well combined. Season with salt and pepper.

Can be stored covered in the refrigerator for up to 3 days.

This favorite in our family is also convenient to make for church service or to make lunch sandwiches. The use of hot dogs may seem different, but it is common in our community. They can be left out, or ground ham could be substituted.

CHURCH PEANUT BUTTER SPREAD

½ cup creamy peanut butter
¼ cup marshmallow crème
1 cup light corn syrup

In a medium mixing bowl, combine the peanut butter, marshmallow crème, and corn syrup. Stir with a rubber spatula until the mixture is smooth and evenly combined.

Place the mixture in a covered container and refrigerate overnight, or 8–12 hours. Allow the spread to come to room temperature before serving on bread or over ice cream.

This recipe is multiplied quite a lot when we host church services. I never eat plain peanut butter, but when mixed like this, I enjoy it.

HOMEMADE CHURCH CHEESE SPREAD

6 pounds process cheese spread (Velveeta)
1½ cup butter
8 cups cream

Put all three ingredients in a big roasting pan and bake at 150°F–200°F, stirring every 15 minutes, until all is melted.

Cover with plastic wrap to prevent it from getting a crusty top while cooling. The spread is served on a sandwich with or without meat. It is good just spread on bread with some pickles.

Our family always likes this with their sandwiches.

If I have a lot of cheese spread left over from hosting church services, I will make "haystack supper" to use up the extra. A "haystack" is a variety of vegetables, toppings, and ground beef with taco seasoning. Sometimes it includes layers of crushed saltine crackers, ground beef, rice, shredded lettuce, diced tomatoes, chopped green bell peppers, sliced green onions, crushed tortilla chips, cheese sauce, and salsa.

PICKLED RED BEETS

10 quarts raw beets
5 cups white vinegar
12 cups water
6 cups sugar
4 teaspoons salt

Boil beets until tender, 10–15 minutes, then drain and peel. Mix together vinegar, water, sugar, and salt. If not canning beets, pour brine over beets. Refrigerate until serving.

To can, place tender, peeled beets in clean, hot quart jars. Pour brine into each jar, leaving ½-inch headspace. Wipe jar rims with a dampened paper towel. Adjust lids and process in a boiling-water canner for 10 minutes.

Makes 10 quarts.

Note: Canning times are subject to change according to USDA regulations. For the latest canning times, check your county extension office or the National Center for Home Food Preservation website.

This recipe makes a brine for 10 quarts of beets. If the vinegar is strong, you may adjust the brine ratio to 1 cup vinegar to every 3 cups water.

SWEET DILLS

1 gallon whole dill pickles
3 cups sugar
¾ cup white vinegar
¾ cup water

Drain pickles, discarding juice. Rinse thoroughly in colander, then slice ¼-inch thick and rinse again. Place sugar, vinegar, and water into saucepan and bring to a boil. Boil for 1 minute, stirring occasionally. Cool slightly.

Clean the pickle jar and put the sliced pickles back in it. Pour boiled (and slightly cooled) mixture over pickles. Leave out for 24 hours, then store in refrigerator.

We like eating pickles with sandwiches. We plant a lot of the small pickles to leave whole for making dill pickles.

Amish Wedding Meals

Timothy and Elizabeth
August 14, 2015

AN AMISH WEDDING

On a Sunday in June at church, our oldest daughter, Elizabeth, and her longtime friend Timothy were published to be married. "Getting published" in an Amish congregation means publicly announcing your engagement.

Elizabeth and Timothy had chosen a Friday in August for their wedding day. There is much to do to prepare for a wedding. Of course, the couple and their families begin preparations long before the official engagement is announced.

Elizabeth sewed her wedding dress and her sisters Susan's and Loretta's dresses. Both of us helped sew dresses for her sisters Verena and Lovina, and for myself. We also sewed new shirts for the boys and my husband, Joe. Overall, Elizabeth did most of the sewing, which was a big help!

Timothy's sister made the wedding invitations. The girls and I and some of his family helped to finish making them. The invitations took a lot of time but were very nice.

Many relatives and friends came to help us get ready for the wedding. One day we made noodles using well over two hundred eggs—yolks only. We saved the egg whites and put them in bags in the freezer—they were used to make angel food cakes for the wedding.

We had helpers who washed all the dishes in both my cupboards and corner cupboard. We washed walls and ceilings in our bedrooms, kitchen, living room, and bathroom. Some went out to work in the garden and did weeding and tilling. The younger girls washed the outside porch and railings. These jobs were spread out over several different workdays. Everyone brought something for lunch so I didn't have to take time to make lunch.

We rented a wedding wagon to have enough space and equipment to make all the food. The wedding wagon comes with seven stoves and two sinks, plus all the pots, pans, and dishes you need for the wedding. It also has a big cooler/freezer to put all the food in after it has been prepared. An 8 x 16-foot trailer comes with it, carrying all the tables, shelves, and dishes.

OUR WEDDING DAY

AUGUST 14

2015

TIMOTHY AND ELIZABETH

We had a lot of help to get the tables set for the wedding. The wedding wagon provides enough place settings for 350 people. We had enough room in the new pole barn to seat 350 people at one time, plus the bride, groom, and their four witnesses, who were seated at a corner table, called the *eck*. The wedding wagon, cooler, and trailer with dishes and tables had to be ready to leave at 7:00 a.m. the next day to go to another home for another wedding.

On the day of the wedding, we serve a meal after the services and actual marriage, which are usually all done by noon. The bride and groom usually open their wedding gifts in the afternoon. Then we serve a 5:00 p.m. supper for guests and a 7:00 p.m. supper for the youth and family.

Joe's cousin Samuel started grilling 350 pounds of chicken at 4:00 a.m. on Friday. Around 6:30 a.m., the cooks started arriving to get the other food prepared. Wedding services were held at the home of our neighbors Joas and Susan. Timothy, Elizabeth, and their four witnesses—daughter Susan; her betrothed, Mose; Tim's sister Martha; and her husband, Ernie—left to go to the neighbors' soon after 7:00 a.m.

Elizabeth likes the color burgundy and Timothy likes purple, so those were the wedding colors. Elizabeth got married in a burgundy-colored dress with a white cape and apron. The grooms always wear a black suit and white shirt, as do the male witnesses. Susan and Martha wore purple dresses with white capes and aprons. Family members wore a shade of rose, and the

tablewaiter girls wore another shade of raspberry-colored material. Timothy's mother and I wore dresses of a dark plum color, and some of the helpers wore purple. The cooks all wore dark gray. The men and boys all wore black pants and vests with white shirts. Timothy's nephews wore rose-colored shirts and sharkskin-gray pants. His nieces wore rose-colored dresses. The bride usually picks the colors of the dresses.

Around 11:30 a.m., toward the end of the service, Bishop Leroy asked Timothy and Elizabeth all the marriage vows, which they responded to with "yes." There are six questions that are asked. Then everyone is asked to stand for a prayer for the couple. After the prayer, the bishop takes the hand of the bride, places it in the hand of the bridegroom, and pronounces them husband and wife.

After the service ended around noon, everyone came to our house for the noon meal. We estimated that there were more than 500 people at our home for that meal. Our menu consisted of barbecued chicken, mashed potatoes,

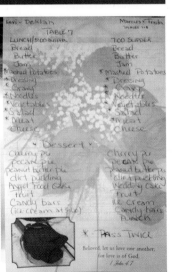

Levi - Delilah   Marcus + Freda

TABLE 7

LUNCH/5:00 SUPPER	7:00 SUPPER
Bread	Bread
Butter	Butter
Jam	Jam
*Mashed Potatoes	*Mashed Potatoes
*Dressing	*Dressing
*Gravy	*Gravy
*Noodles	*Noodles
*Vegetables	*Vegetables
*Salad	*Salad
*Meat	*Meat
*Cheese	*Cheese

* Dessert *

Cherry pie	Cherry pie
Pecan pie	Pecan pie
Peanut butter pie	Peanut butter pie
dirt pudding	dirt pudding
Angel Food Cake	Wedding cake
Fruit	Fruit
Candy bars	Ice cream
(ice cream at 5:00)	Candy bars
	Punch

* - PASS TWICE

Beloved, let us love one another,
for love is of God.
1 John 4:7

gravy, noodles, dressing, corn, cheese, lettuce salad, homemade bread, butter, strawberry jam, angel food cake (with frosting and Danish dessert topping), dirt pudding, mixed fruit, and pies—cherry, pecan, and peanut butter. We made twenty-five of each kind of pie. Candy bars were passed around after the meal. The same menu was served at night, but smoked sausage and ice cream were added to the menu. We served around 575 people for supper.

Timothy and Elizabeth opened their gifts in the afternoon. They received a lot of nice gifts to add to their new home. The gifts are usually household items such as kitchen items, towels, and bedding, and some give things like tools and shovels for the groom. Money is given by some who aren't sure what to give, which is nice because the bride and groom can go buy other necessities.

One of my "English" friends, Ruth, who also helped with this cookbook, helped us out so much before the wedding. She went and got whatever we ran out of or forgot. She took me shopping, one trip after another, to get the many groceries needed for the wedding. She also did loads of laundry for me when we had rainy weather. She washed all the towels and dishcloths after each meal. I don't know how I can ever repay her. A true friend indeed! Thanks so much, Ruth, and all the many helpers who got things ready and cooked or served on the day of the wedding.

My thoughts and prayers were with my firstborn as I thought of her taking this big step in life. She will have a lot of changes, but I have no doubt in my mind that they will be good ones. It is just a mother's nature to worry for her children, but there needs to be a time to let them experience life without the presence of their parents.

Elizabeth and Timothy, may you have a long and happy married life together. May God grant you both good health and a family to love. My love to both of you.

—*Lovina Eicher*

All the quantities listed in this "Amish Wedding Meals" chapter are for typical Amish weddings, but some need to be multiplied depending on the number of expected guests. Amish weddings vary greatly from one community to the next and have different traditions, practices, and foods. The size of containers used for cooking would vary greatly also, depending on what the families helping with the cooking have available to use, and what would be available in the wedding wagon of supplies that many families are able to rent for a wedding.

ANGEL FOOD CAKE

2 cups egg whites, beaten until foamy

1 teaspoon cream of tartar

1 teaspoon salt

1 teaspoon almond extract

1 cup granulated sugar, sifted

1 cup pastry or cake flour

1 cup powdered sugar

Combine egg whites, cream of tartar, salt, and almond extract. Beat in granulated sugar until stiff peaks form. Sift together flour and powdered sugar. Gradually fold flour mixture into egg white mixture. Pour into a non-greased tube pan. Bake at 350°F for 45 minutes, or until cake feels springy.

Tip: *To more easily remove cake from a tube pan, use waxed or parchment paper cut to fit the bottom of the pan. When the cake is baked, use knife or scraper to cut around the sides of the cake and the pan, then turn the pan upside down. The cake should slide out easily. If the cake has risen higher than the pan during baking, some turn it upside down on a bottle to cool and to remove it from the pan.*

Some people prefer angel food cakes at weddings; others prefer sheet cakes. I let Elizabeth choose which one they wanted at their wedding. The angel food cakes are usually cut in half horizontally to make two cakes out of one. This reduces the size of each piece to half. With all the good food at weddings, a small slice of cake is enough.

FROSTING FOR ANGEL FOOD CAKE

8 cups powdered sugar
4 (8-ounce) packages cream cheese
4 (16-ounce) containers frozen whipped topping, thawed

Mix together powdered sugar and cream cheese. Fold whipped topping into mixture. Spread on cakes and top with Danish Topping. Enough to frost four cakes.

DANISH TOPPING

1¾ cup fruit juice or water, divided
1 (3-ounce) package flavored gelatin (any flavor)
⅓ cup sugar
¼ cup cornstarch or Clear Jel
1 quart fresh strawberries, sliced; or canned fruit, drained

Heat 1 cup juice or water to boiling. Separately, combine remaining ¾ cup juice or water, flavored gelatin, sugar, and cornstarch or Clear Jel. Add gelatin mixture to boiling liquid, and cook about 1 minute. Pour mixture over fruit. Stir to blend; refrigerate until ready to serve. Pour over frosted Angel Food Cake.

Tip: Some brides or families make the topping colorful using their choice of gelatin flavor for whatever colors they have chosen for their wedding.

BREAD

2½ cups warm water
2 heaping tablespoons active dry yeast
1 teaspoon sugar
7 cups hot water
1 cup vegetable oil
1½ cup additional sugar
4 tablespoons salt
About 26 cups flour

In a small bowl, stir together the warm water, yeast, and 1 teaspoon sugar. In a large bowl, stir together the hot water, oil, 1½ cup additional sugar, and salt.

Add 2–4 cups flour to the hot liquid, beating well, then add the yeast mixture. Gradually add the rest of the flour. Stir until soft dough is formed; let rise in bowl until doubled.

Divide dough to make about 10 small loaves, using greased 7 x 3-inch loaf pans, 1¼ pound dough per pan. Let rise in pans until doubled in size.

Bake at 350°F for 20-25 minutes, or until golden brown.

Twenty loaves are enough for most weddings, especially with all the other food prepared.

DRESSING

Bread crumbs:

1 cup butter, melted

2 gallons toasted bread crumbs

Recipe:

16 eggs, beaten

2 quarts chicken broth and meat (about ¼ of total is meat)

1 quart carrots, shredded

1 quart celery, diced

1½ quarts potatoes, cooked and diced (reserve 1 quart cooking water)

1 pint onions, diced

To pour over dressing:

2 quarts milk

1 quart water (reserved from cooking potatoes, or plain water)

2 teaspoons black pepper

3 tablespoons chicken base

Pour butter over bread crumbs in large mixing bowl. Let stand. In another bowl, beat eggs. Add eggs to bread crumbs and butter. Add chicken broth and meat, carrots, celery, potatoes, onions, milk, water, pepper, chicken base. Stir all together until mixed. Use clean hands to mix if necessary. Put stirred dressing into roaster or large pan. In separate bowl, stir milk, water, pepper, and chicken base together. Pour over dressing before baking.

One batch makes enough for about one large roaster. Or use large size alumunim foil disposable pans, 14½ x 10⅝-inch size. To make clean up easier if you plan to wash and save disposable pans, line bottom of pan with parchment paper. Makes about 13 quarts.

Bake at 350°F for one hour, or until set when you shake the pan.

MASHED POTATOES

Shopping list for about 10 pots peeled potatoes:

3 pounds butter

10 (8-ounce) packages cream cheese (optional)

10 quarts milk

Cooking and quantities needed:

8 (8-quart) pots potatoes (for wedding guests)

2 (8-quart) pots potatoes (for cooks and extras, about 50 people)

6 teaspoons salt

3 pounds butter

10 (8-ounce) packages cream cheese (optional)

10 quarts milk, heated (don't scorch or burn)

Boil potatoes in salted water until cooked through, 25–30 minutes. Drain potatoes (you may wish to reserve water to use in gravy, dressing, or noodles). Mash potatoes well, then add butter; add cream cheese, if desired. Mash potatoes well again, then gradually stir in heated milk. (Adding the milk all at once will make lumpy potatoes.)

For our oldest daughter's wedding, we bought 400 pounds of potatoes, and I think we didn't use about 75 of those pounds. When we lived near Berne, Indiana, all the potatoes, even for weddings, were mashed by hand. For our daughter's wedding, the wedding wagon we rented was set up with a generator to produce power to use mixers to make the mashed potatoes and other items.

I like using cream cheese in the potatoes; my mother only used butter because I think she thought adding cream cheese was too expensive. But when I married Joe, I learned from his grandmother what a delicious richness it added. She also told me that it helps take out the lumps when you mash them by hand. When we make mashed potatoes just for the family, we mash them with a hand-masher.

GRAVY, VERSION 1

BROWN GRAVY WITH CHICKEN BROTH

4 quarts water

Scant ½ cup chicken soup base

1¾ pound butter

4 cups flour

1 teaspoon salt

2 teaspoons pepper, or to taste

In a large pot, heat water to boiling. Add soup base and stir broth until dissolved.

In another large (8-quart) pot, melt butter over medium heat. Brown the butter by continuing to cook over medium heat. The butter will start to foam and turn brown. Stir occasionally through this process—it can burn very easily, so watch carefully. Once the butter is browned, add the flour, 1 cup at a time. Using a whisk or a spatula, mix the butter with the flour until a paste is formed.

Once a paste is formed, add the hot broth. Cook over medium heat, stirring constantly for 10–15 minutes, until gravy becomes thick. Add salt and pepper.

GRAVY, VERSION 2

EGG GRAVY

2 quarts chicken broth

2 quarts water

6 egg yolks, beaten

15 tablespoons flour

3 tablespoons chicken soup base

Salt and pepper, to taste

Put broth and water into a 6-quart pot. Separately, combine egg yolks, flour, and cold water to make a smooth paste. Pour paste into boiling broth, stirring briskly. Add chicken soup base. Season with salt and pepper.

AMISH NOODLES

1 quart chicken broth

3–3½ cups small cut up chicken pieces, cooked

4 pounds noodles

7 quarts potato water, if available; or plain water

1 cup chicken soup base

1 tablespoon salt

Bring broth and chicken pieces to a boil in 12-quart kettle; stir in noodles. Add potato water, chicken soup base, and salt. Return to a full boil and cook for several minutes, then turn off heat. Cover and let stand for 30 minutes.

MEAT LOAF

40 pounds ground beef

1 quart onions, finely chopped

25 cups cracker crumbs

33 eggs, beaten

4 quarts tomato juice

4 tablespoons Worcestershire sauce

3 tablespoons salt

1 tablespoon pepper

Combine all ingredients, mixing thoroughly. Divide into numerous 9 x 11-inch large loaf pans as needed. Or, put two large meat loaves into one roaster, as many roasters as needed. Bake at 350°F for 1¼ hour. (With multiple pans in the oven, the loaves may need more time, and a hotter oven.)

Makes enough for 250 people.

PIE DOUGH

6 cups flour (pastry flour works best)
2 teaspoons baking powder
1 teaspoon salt
2 cups lard
2 eggs
⅔ cup water
2 teaspoons vinegar

Mix together flour, baking powder, and salt. Add lard and cut with a pastry cutter or two forks until crumbs are formed. It's best if crumbs are quite moist—add a little more lard if necessary.

Beat together eggs, water, and vinegar and pour over crumb mixture. Mix with a fork until right consistency. Do not overmix.

Makes 6 pie crusts (for 3 pies, top and bottom crusts; or for 6 pies, single crusts).

PEANUT BUTTER PIE

8 cups milk

2 cups granulated sugar

1⅓ cup flour

¼ teaspoon salt

3 eggs, beaten

4 (9-inch) pie shells, baked

Whipped topping

Crumbs

9 cups powdered sugar

3 cups peanut butter

Heat milk to scalding. In a separate bowl, mix granulated sugar, flour, salt, and eggs. Add mixture to hot milk and cook over medium heat, stirring constantly, until thick. Remove from heat.

Make crumbs: Stir together the powdered sugar and peanut butter until it has a crumbly texture. Place ¾ cup of this crumb mixture into bottom of each baked pie shell. Reserve the remaining crumbs for topping.

Divide cooked mixture among pie shells. Let pies cool, then refrigerate.

When ready to serve, top with whipped topping and sprinkle the remaining crumbs evenly over the four pies.

Makes 4 (9-inch) pies.

POOR MAN'S STEAK

To serve 350–400:

40 pounds ground beef

3½ quarts cracker crumbs

3½ cups milk

4 tablespoons plus 2 teaspoons salt

2 tablespoons plus 1 teaspoon pepper

2 quarts onions, chopped

Per each 3 pounds ground beef, 1 (10¾-ounce) can condensed cream of mushroom soup

To serve 450–500:

50 pounds ground beef

4 quarts cracker crumbs

4 cups milk

5 tablespoons plus 1 teaspoon salt

3 tablespoons pepper

2½ quarts onions

Per each 3 pounds ground beef, 1 (10¾-ounce) can condensed cream of mushroom soup

Mix ground beef, cracker crumbs, milk, salt, pepper, and onions in large container. Place meat mixture on big baking sheets, and top with mushroom soup mixed with milk (see below) before baking.

To pour over top: Use 1 (10¾-ounce) can cream of mushroom soup per 3 pounds meat. Mix with milk and pour over burger. Bake uncovered at 350°F for 45-60 minutes.

A lot of people grill or fry Poor Man's Steak like burgers. We usually put the ground beef in one layer on a big baking sheet, and refrigerate it to bake the next day; we put the rest of the mixture on top just before baking.

AMISH WEDDING NOTHINGS, OR KNEE PATCHES

3 large "cookspoons" heavy cream (¾ cup)
1 egg, well beaten
pinch salt
2 cups flour
Shortening, for frying
Sugar, for topping

Stir together cream, egg, salt, and enough flour to make an elastic dough. Make 7–9 balls out of the dough. Roll out each ball of dough very flat and thin, about ¹⁄₁₆ inch. Cut six three-inch slits, one above the other, in the middle of each round of dough.

Heat shortening in a large pot over high heat (or use an electric skillet with a temperature control). When the shortening is 365°F, drop in small piece of dough to see if it cooks or sizzles. When oil is hot enough, put the rolled-out dough into the pot or skillet. (Fry one at a time, unless you have a huge kettle.) When it turns golden on the bottom, turn once with two forks or large spatula. Remove from pot and drain on plate covered with paper towels.

Sprinkle powdered sugar over top while warm. To serve, stack the nothings on top of one another on a plate.

One batch makes 7–9 nothings. For a wedding, we would make 12–15 batches, or more as needed.

A second daughter, Susan, married in August 2016. We enjoyed making "nothings" for guests, which was a tradition my family had when we lived in another community. Nothings are a thin rolled-out pastry, deep-fried, sprinkled with sugar, and stacked on top of one another. They are delicious!

INDEX

ABOUT THE AUTHOR

Lovina Eicher is author of the syndicated column Lovina's Amish Kitchen, which appears in forty newspapers around the United States and on a weekly blog. She is the author of several cookbooks. Lovina and her husband have eight children and live in rural Michigan.

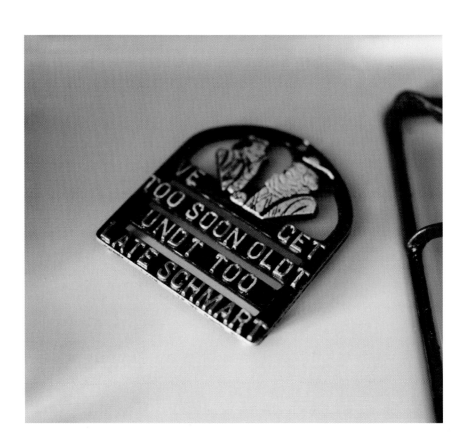